DESIGNING & OPERATING
YARDS

Dave Abeles

ACKNOWLEDGEMENTS:

    A great deal of life is upon us in the dynamic years of the 2020s, and I am grateful for the support, assistance, and guidance of of so many people at this point in my writing. It is difficult to overstate the patience and amazing railroad operations mind of Jack Trabachino, a best friend for more than 35 years and one of the "wisdom keepers" of the Onondaga Cutoff. For this work, the idea came from the staff at Firecrown and specifically *Model Railroader* Editor Eric White, whose editing skills and guidance with my many questions benefitted everything I have written here. Early on in this writing Tony Koester and Jerry Dziedzic offered resources and support, while Lionel Strang and Heath Hofmeister offered encouragement to take on the challenge of another book project. Mark Hemphill's extensive research and prototype experience provided rich information as well as inspiration to make this writing as true to the prototype as possible. Once again, proofreads by Rich Wisneski and Joe Relation were critical to the flow and accuracy of the text. Noted OC Yardmaster Al Tillotson helped with text and photos, as did Ralph Heiss. The most critical part of this work, however, is the foundation of stable home and loving family that is maintained by my wife Kristen, whose smiling support and patient intelligence surround me. The energy and life that flows out of children Susie, Teddy, and Pete is dynamic and fulfilling, adding color to my world which is woven throughout this text. So many people added to this work and I am grateful for each of them and for the spirit for which I am a conduit. The contributions and success of this work are in large part due to them and a tribute to the community, while any mistakes belong to me alone.

    May the best be yet to come!

Dave Abeles

On the cover: Conrail freight COSE with run-through CN power has arrived at Onondaga Yard on Dave Abeles' HO scale Onondaga Cutoff, while yard job YAON-14 works alongside classifying cars bound for different destinations. Classification is a central theme at railroad yards.

Back cover: Top left: Onandaga Yard is the operational hub of Dave Abeles' layout. Top right: A locomotive eases onto the turntable at Bessemer Yard on Lou Steenwyk's HO Ashland & Iron River. Bottom right: Doug Watts works the east end of Frankfort Yard on Tony Koester's multideck HO Nickel Plate Road layout.

Firecrown
605 Chestnut Street, Suite 800
Chattanooga, TN 37450

Shop.Trains.com

© 2024 Dave Abeles
All rights reserved. This book may not be reproduced in part or in whole by any means whether electronic or otherwise without written permission of the publisher except for brief excerpts for review.

All photos by the author unless otherwise noted.

Published in 2024
28 27 26 25 24   1 2 3 4 5

Manufactured in China

ISBN: 979-8-89491-002-4
EISBN: 979-8-89491-003-1

Editor: Jeff Wilson
Book Design: Lisa Schroeder

CONTENTS

Introduction:
The fascination of railroad yards.............................4

Chapter 1 8
Freight yard history and development

Chapter 2 18
Waterfront and other terminal yards

Chapter 3 32
Classification yards

Chapter 4 44
Blocking operations

Chapter 5 54
Yard design: Your layout and its mission

Chapter 6 66
Yard design and construction

Chapter 7 80
Car forwarding and staging yards

Chapter 8 88
Modeling maintenance areas

Chapter 9 96
The yardmaster: setting the pace

Chapter 10 108
A last look at yards

Modeled yard operations bear a lot of resemblance to yard operations on the prototype. Cars arrive, are classified, and then assembled for pickup by outbound trains, all under close coordination of the yardmaster. Joe Relation, left, and Ralph Heiss work together at Onondaga Yard on my HO scale Onondaga Cutoff, which represents Conrail's 1994-era Chicago Line in central New York state.

INTRODUCTION

THE FASCINATION OF RAILROAD YARDS

"Railroad yard" is a term that is extremely evocative of railroading, and full of potential for railfans and modelers alike. What comes to mind when you imagine a railroad yard? Busy switchers and a sea of freight cars spread across dozens of parallel tracks, **1**? Or perhaps a fleet of passenger cars, all serviced and ready for another trip across the country, **2**? What about a few cars on weed-grown tracks at the end of a branch line, **3**?

The differences in these types of yards may be readily apparent, but their similarity defines the very essence of railroading. How can these different images be correlated?

Denver & Rio Grande Western SW1500 No. 144 switches a long line of Rio Grande insulated boxcars at the railroad's home base, North Yard in Denver, Colo. Al Tillotson

While much has changed through the years, some operating concepts remain constant and vital, and one of the most foundational is that of the railroad yard.

Nowhere else on the railroad will so many trains pause for attention, and nowhere else can you find a such a thorough cross-section of a railroad, its people, and its operations. Many professional railroaders report to a yard for their work. Trains are taken apart and reassembled, cars are sorted for destinations across the continent, and locomotives and cars alike are inspected and serviced, **4**. Crews come and go as they board and climb down from locomotives and, in past days, cabooses. Passenger trains are assembled, **5**, and made ready. Specialized intermodal yards both classify trains and serve as points where containers and piggyback trailers enter and leave the rail network as they switch from rail to highway or ship transport.

And yet, yard designs and the specific physical plant vary as much as anything else in the industry over its history. You may be familiar with the different forms, but you may not be — perhaps you're seeing these concepts for the first time. All of us interested in railroading can learn to appreciate the wide array of yard designs and functions.

Yards, along with every other category of railroad facility, are built and maintained at great expense solely for the reason the railroad itself exists: efficiently moving goods and people from one place to another.

WHAT ARE YARDS AND WHAT DO THEY DO?

The short answer is that yards serve as a railcar sorting, classification, and distribution system, all in one. Think of it like the postal service: items are gathered, sorted, and re-routed to finish their journeys. Each car on a railroad is likewise gathered, sorted, and routed toward its destination. Railroads revolutionized transportation, and the yard has always been the industry's faithful servant: the place where trains converge to exchange cars, people, and goods before continuing to a final destination.

You can model yards no matter the size, era, or region of your layout, and this book is your key to understanding how. We will discuss how yards came to be, how they have survived nearly 200 years of rail history, and why they remain so critical even in the 21st century. Like prototype yards, your modeled yards will have unique features that both help and hinder its purpose, and yet yours can function successfully and be an enjoyable part of your model railroad. In all but the largest cases, we deal with less available real estate than the prototype and, as a result, our designs must be adjusted.

My goal is to show you an overview of how prototype yards are built, organized, and run. We'll then examine a

2 Passenger cars and facilities stretch nearly to the horizon at the Terminal Railroad Association of St. Louis coach yards on April 20, 1965. The TRRA served St. Louis Union Station, once one of the country's busiest passenger terminals. Rich Taylor

3 A few tracks at the end of a short line is a yard, too, weeds or not. Euclid Yard on the Minoa & Euclid — a short line connecting to Conrail on my HO layout — is switched by Morristown & Erie Alcos on Sept. 15, 1994.

variety of successful model railroads, which will allow your imagination to work on applying concepts to your specific situation. We will take this cross-section and examine yard operations in detail on a variety of different prototypes and work to understand how their principles can be adapted to our modeled world. Operations takes center stage as the book continues and we move into different types of modeled activity and see how we can orchestrate that on our physical plant. We will look hard at variations such as staging yards that exist on our layouts in order to represent the world beyond our model railroads.

If this all sounds like a lot to tackle, it is — there's a lot to think through. Let this book be your guide to understanding and execution of design concepts to accomplish enjoyable operation and pleasing aesthetics on your layout, **6**.

Model yards have a huge aesthetic and operational impact on any layout. This book will help you build a foundation for why yards and yard operation matter so much and the foundation will serve you well into the future, bringing your railroad to life.

St. Marys Yard on Perry Squier's beautiful HO scale Pittsburg, Shawmut & Northern represents everything about its prototype. The yard is the center of operations. Coal was king and other traffic filled the gaps; the company stenciled "Shawmut" on everything it could.

A chilly Oct. 8, 2023, night finds NJ Transit ALP46 No. 4640 in its heritage paint scheme laying over at Amtrak's Sunnyside Yard in Long Island City, N.Y. Sunnyside, one of the largest passenger train facilities in North America, was a 192-acre Pennsylvania Railroad creation that is just as relevant in today as it was a hundred years ago. Lou Capwell

Cayuga, Ind., on Tony Koester's HO scale Nickel Plate Road, is a small town with big operational impact. Here big NKP Berkshire 789 glides through town on a superelevated curve past the track department office while local cars await spotting in the yard tracks.

CHAPTER ONE

1 Train 43 gets underway from the massive yards at Frankfort, Ind., stepping out onto the main line of Tony Koester's incredible HO Nickel Plate Road Cloverleaf Subdivision layout. Frankfort has an eastbound and westbound yard and Berkshire No. 707 wastes no time getting the train underway.

FREIGHT YARD HISTORY AND DEVELOPMENT

Railroads exist to move goods and people safely and look to do so in as cost-effective a manner as possible. Railroads require a great deal of infrastructure, people, equipment, and effort to make transportation happen. Since railroads invest a lot of time, effort, and money in designing, building, and operating their yards, it follows that the railroad yard is a big part of the transportation story.

2

From railroads' beginnings to today, extra tracks have been needed where trains pass. Here BNSF trains with trackage rights over host Montana Rail Link pass at Livingston, Mont., on September 29, 2014, with the huge Livingston shop complex in the distance. Crews are also working to add another siding track to help with the growing export coal business on MRL's former Northern Pacific main line. MRL has since become part of BNSF.

Simply put, yards exist not to store cars but instead as part of an integrated network created to efficiently move cars to their destinations, **1**. A key term is *move*. Railroads are for moving things. Cars are not intended to sit in a yard unless it's specifically designed for storage. Cars are in yards on a temporary basis to be rearranged before going somewhere else. Railroads get paid when loaded cars are delivered.

This is a key piece of information to keep in mind as we proceed. While this book will look at the design, construction, and operation of model railroad yards, we must start with the prototype in order to understand why and how yards exist and what they do.

What makes railroads unique is that the rails themselves guide all movements. Locomotives and cars have no steering mechanism besides their flanged wheels and the rails on which they roll. This seems basic, but in truth has important ramifications and indeed is the foundation of yard design and operation, as locomotives and cars can only more forward and back and can only pass each other on separate tracks, **2**. Passing another car or train requires a parallel siding or track, even if only a single-ended spur where equipment can rest while another move passes.

On the first railroads, one car or set of cars could be moved from one end of the line to the other. Once owners realized that more freight could be moved with a second car or set of cars, a method was needed for allowing them to pass in the middle of the route — enter the turnout and a second (passing) track. Additional tracks were then added at the ends of the line as well, where cars could be shunted aside for loading or unloading. Obviously, a

9

Early railroads quickly became affiliated with waterways to move freight to inland points. Bernard Kempinski scratchbuilt an O scale steam tug and carfloat for his Civil War United States Military Railroad. In 1862 General Herman Haupt, superintendent of the USMRR, instituted a carfloat operation on the Potomac River to run from Alexandria, Va., to Aquia Landing, 60 miles to the south. The floats were built by joining two barges. Long timbers were placed crosswise from the float's bow, supporting eight tracks. Bernard Kempinski

third track would in turn allow loading or storage of more cars — the pattern was clear. These primitive "terminals" quickly grew in size and importance, becoming the genesis of what we know today as the railroad yard.

OPPORTUNITY AND EARLY OPERATION

The key locations on the early railroad network were, predictably, the direct access points to canals and seaports or to tidewater. When labor was cheap, the arduous task of transloading freight from rail cars to barges and ships was done almost entirely by hand and was a very cost-effective — albeit slow — way of moving freight, **3**. Still, the faster that freight cars cycle into, through, and out of a yard, the better for revenue.

As early railroads grew and began to serve different industries and destinations, yard operation became more diverse. Cars still gathered for outbound trains to other destinations and cabooses were added. Brakemen walked between freight cars on yard tracks, "pulling the pin" of the link-and-pin coupler systems and using hand signals to guide locomotive engineers and build outbound trains. Yards allowed for a great increase in efficient car movement — trains from several origins could bring cars to a yard along the route, at which point the cars in the train would be yarded and "classified" — sorted according to destination.

Steam engines went to the engine house to be watered and refueled, **4**, cabooses were sent to a dedicated track to be cleaned and restocked, and then fresh engines and cabooses were reassigned to outbound trains with new crews. Freight cars, now in a train classified by destination, would move on.

Yards at the ends of routes were originally level and stub-ended, serving specific needs and traffic types. Early rulebooks define a yard as "a system of tracks within defined limits provided for the making up of trains over which movements not authorized by timetable or special instruction may operate according to the prescribed rules." This means a locomotive could move as needed within the confines of the yard without special permission. The yard locomotive moved cars around the yard and sorted them by outbound destinations, working from the ladder end of the yard. This process worked, but it was labor intensive and required a lot of locomotives to handle different jobs. As traffic increased and yards became larger, single-ended yards rapidly fell out of favor. Improvements included double-ended yards, typically developed away from congested waterfronts. These increased efficiency by allowing classification from both ends simultaneously, but the intensity of manual operation still had its limits, **5**.

In the latter part of the 19th century, operating territories or divisions (the distance a road crew ran one train in a day) generally were about 100 miles. Since train speeds rarely exceeded 25 miles an hour for freight traffic and many stops were made along the way, 100 miles was about

Engine facilities were commonly located adjacent to freight yards in the steam era, as seen on John Paganoni's HO version of the Central Vermont's New London Yard. Here CV 451 is pulling empties for the next outbound train. In the background, the roundhouse crew is ready to bring out a road engine. John scratchbuilt the roundhouse with a highly detailed interior and lighting. Mat Thompson

a full day of hard labor. Nearly every car was classified at every yard along the way, and as traffic increased in the 1880s and 1890s, the bigger yards were switching huge volumes of cars multiple times.

Like so much on the railroad, a more efficient way to handle classification was just an idea away. By the 1880s, several yards in Great Britain and Germany were being built to take advantage of one of the earth's few constants: gravity. The idea behind the "gravity yard," which was the predecessor to today's hump yards, seems simple in hindsight but was revolutionary at the time. Cars were pushed up an artificial hill, uncoupled by crews at the apex, and then rolled by gravity downgrade through switches onto a number of parallel tracks. Each of these tracks was ramped back up on the far side so cars would slow to a stop in the middle, creating a "bowl" profile. Blocks of cars or whole trains could be assembled this way in far less time than was required for locomotives to manually move each car.

THE NEXT STEP: HUMP YARDS

By 1900, railroads (and rail traffic) were growing quickly. Although grav-

Pittsburg, Shawmut & Northern extra 74 north is arriving at St. Marys Yard on a late summer day in 1923, where its cars will be sorted for outbound trains. This yard is a flat-switching facility with ladder tracks on both ends of the yard to increase efficiency.

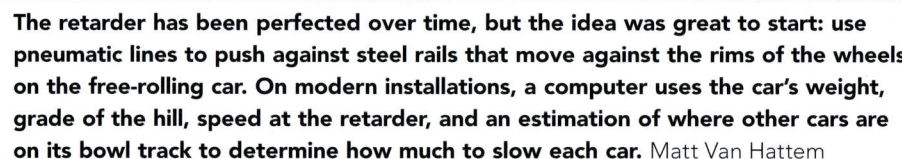

The retarder has been perfected over time, but the idea was great to start: use pneumatic lines to push against steel rails that move against the rims of the wheels on the free-rolling car. On modern installations, a computer uses the car's weight, grade of the hill, speed at the retarder, and an estimation of where other cars are on its bowl track to determine how much to slow each car. Matt Van Hattem

7 Two hump locomotives — SD38-2 UPY No. 805 and SD40-2 UP No. 3267 — have completed their task of shoving cars over the west hump at UP's Bailey Yard. A crew member (left), stationed at the crest of the hump, controls the locomotives remotely using a beltpack while uncoupling cars.
Two photos: Matt Van Hattem

8 From the West Hump yard tower at Union Pacific's huge Bailey Yard in North Platte, Neb., yardmaster Gale Malcolm manages train classifications in the westbound classification yard, one of the two hump yards situated within the eight-mile-long, two-mile-wide terminal. Matt Van Hattem

9 The switchman receives uncoupling directions via radio from a foreman in the west hump yard tower, who also remotely lines the switches to direct cars rolling down the hump into the correct bowl tracks. The height of Bailey's West Hump is 20.1 feet. Matt Van Hattem

10 Powered by gravity, boxcars roll down Bailey Yard's west hump. The westbound classification yard has 49 tracks. Cars can be sent over the hump in cuts of one or two loaded cars or up to three empty cars. As cars roll down the hump, radar detectors measure their speed so retarders can apply the proper amount of force to slow the car for a 1.6-mph coupling. Matt Van Hattem

ity yards were efficient, there were problems, especially as train lengths increased and cars became heavier. Differing weights of cars, changing temperatures, varying rates of rolling resistance, and wind conditions could all affect the speed of any particular car as it coasted downgrade. Some cars stopped too soon; others went too fast and collided heavily with other cars on the track. A system was needed to control the speed (and therefore the inertia) of both loaded and empty cars. While sources differ over the exact location, it is evident that the world's largest railroad at the time — the mighty Pennsylvania Railroad — was a leader in building and operating the first hump yard in the world.

The PRR had developed an extensive system of yards and experimented with the concept of a man-made hump of earth, steeply graded, over which incoming cars were pushed. At the top,

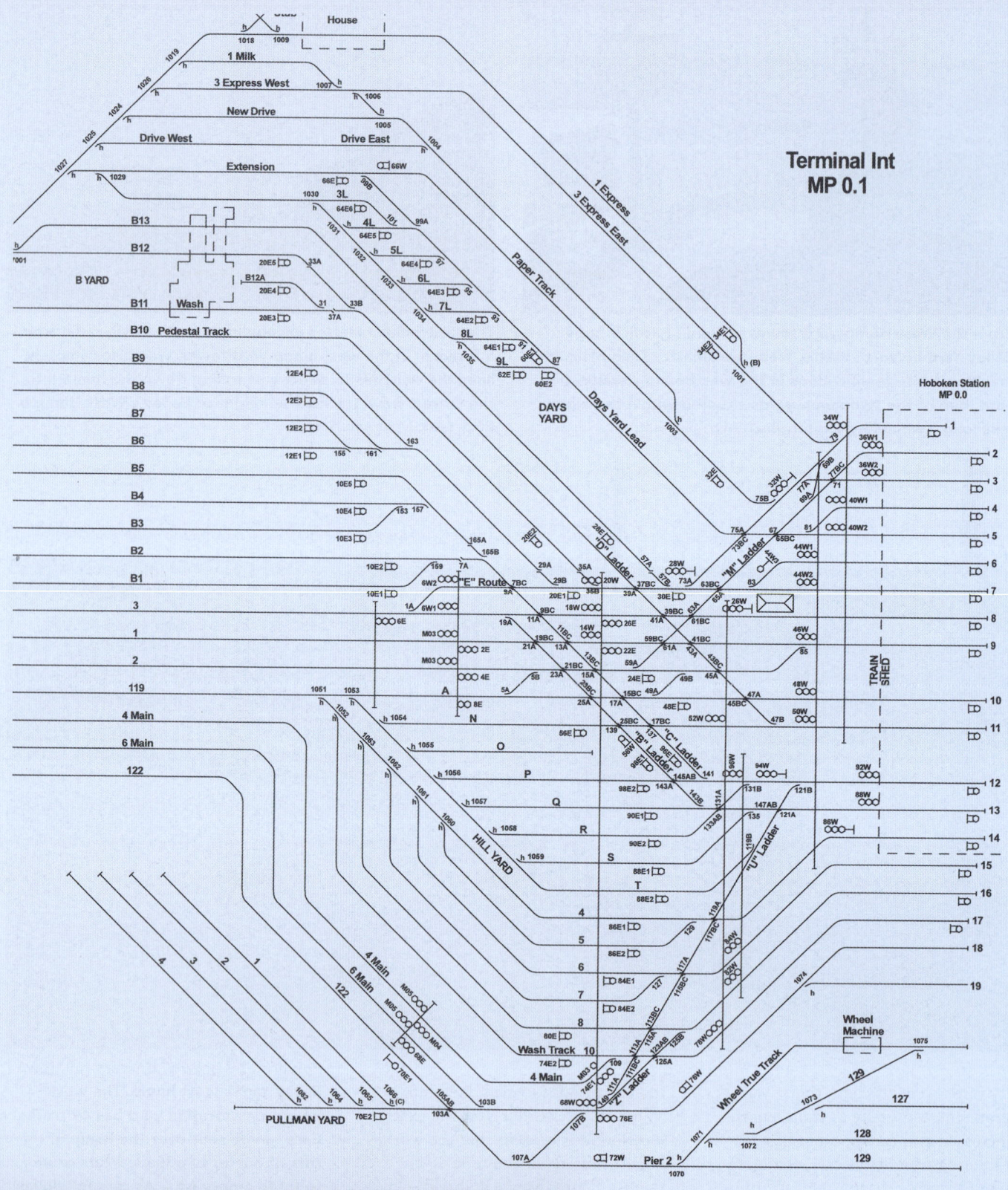

Hoboken Terminal and its associated yard trackage was built by the Delaware, Lackawanna & Western and used subsequently by the Erie, then Erie Lackawanna, Conrail, and now NJ Transit. This sprawling facility includes full passenger-car servicing facilities and works to support the vast system of commuter trains in New Jersey.

like a gravity yard, cars were uncoupled and rolled downgrade by gravity through a series of switches. However, PRR figured out that by adding a braking system on the downgrade tracks leading to the bowl, workers could manually slow the cars to control the speed. These devices, called "retarders," clamped on the wheel rims as the cars rolled through the retarder, **6**. The retarders and switches were initially operated manually, but later systems allowed control from a tower built alongside the hump, **7, 8**. Double-ended classification bowls then allowed assembled cuts to be pulled from the opposite end of the hump for assembly into outbound trains.

As larger and more complex operations developed, freight yards grew larger, with multiple areas for different tasks: arrival yard, hump, classification yard, and departure yard; engine, caboose, and car-servicing facilities; and repair shops. The largest and most modern freight classification yards were built with all of these elements and designed from the start with each component working in concert with the rest. We'll examine classification yards in detail in Chapter 3, but take a quick look at one of the largest and most important hump operations in the world today: Union Pacific's facility at Bailey Yard, in North Platte, Neb., **9, 10**.

PASSENGER YARDS

Unlike freight trains, where cars are switched into and out of nearly every train, many passenger trains essentially run as "sets" — the same cars stay coupled and run back and forth over the line, **11**. Therefore, early passenger trains would simply "turn" at the destination, with the engine spinning on a turntable or wye, **12**. The train too could be turned on a wye if the leads were long enough. Failing that, the coaches and other cars would simply be pulled in the opposite direction for the next run.

Dedicated passenger yards began to develop by the mid-1800s as runs became longer, trains became longer, and routings became more complicated, **13**. These provided tracks for

Toronto has long been a hub for passenger trains. The unique VIA Rail TurboTrain ran for years through the city and was double-ended, facilitating turns and servicing. Here Turbo No. 126 is fueled at the Spadina Yard facilities on August 14, 1979. Rich Taylor

Like steam locomotives, cab-unit diesels need to face forward to run most (non push-pull) passenger trains, and a turntable was a space-efficient way to do it. Erie Lackawanna E8A No. 824 rolls off the table to a service track at the sprawling former Delaware, Lackawanna & Western facility at Hoboken, N.J., on April 9, 1971. Rich Taylor

Extensive trackwork was common in passenger yards, especially in pre-Amtrak days. The terminal at St. Louis was known for the incredible number of railroads it served, with subsequently complicated trackwork; 32 stub-ended tracks terminated under its 600-foot-wide shed (at right). New York Central Train 312, The *Southwestern*, departs St. Louis for Cleveland on April 20, 1965. Rich Taylor

15 The Central Railroad of New Jersey built a large shop complex at Elizabethport, N.J., near its eastern terminus. The CNJ is long gone and many of its lines are no longer part of through routes, but even in 2023 the old yard serves an important role for local freight traffic and as a transload facility for local trucks.

14 Passenger yards require another layer of car servicing compared to freight yards, and extra facilities are required. Canadian National GP40 4106 rolls past Cabin D at Bathhurst Street in Toronto as it positions itself for service and another run. Rich Taylor

MODERNIZED YARDS

Selkirk Yard (below), built in 1968 as the New York Central railroad worked to automate and streamline its systemwide classification system, is still a vital link in the North American rail network. Elkhart Yard in Elkhart, Ind. (right) was modernized at the same time as part of the wise vision of NYC President Al Perlman. Conrail in the 1980s created visitor guidebooks for these and other yards to help the public understand their significance. Conrail

16 Yards can be an important focus of our model railroads just as they are on the prototype. Joe Binish has captured the busy look of a late-steam, early diesel yard on his HO layout. Rich Remiarz

storing cars between runs and for the more extensive servicing of passenger equipment, which required car interior and exterior cleaning, window washing, minor repairs to customer amenities, and by the 1900s, maintenance and restocking of dining car kitchens as well as maintaining air conditioning, **14**. Parts of yards developed their own names as identity from the other facilities in the yard (see the Hoboken Terminal map on page 14).

PLANNING AND EVOLUTION

As we have seen so far, a good majority of early railroads and their yard facilities developed organically — local need drove growth from a few tracks to larger and larger facilities. Then as now, one of the greatest challenges in railroading is upgrading and expanding yard facilities under traffic. Railroads in the early part of the 20th century had their sights set on dominating certain service lanes and markets and the largest of these — major western roads as well as eastern trunk lines — created sophisticated planning departments that looked at operational flow of traffic and made decisions on the huge investments needed to improve operations. Better efficiency was required to compete with trucks; but even after the creation of the Interstate highway system, trains move tonnage long distances more cheaply than trucks, so yards continue to be vital, **15**.

Much information exists on the grandest examples of yards, those on the largest Class I railroads that were constructed or improved through the 1930s and later into the 1950s. Santa Fe rebuilt an entirely new hump yard at Barstow, Calif., the location where trains coming from the east would turn south to head toward Los Angeles via Cajon Pass or directly west to head over Tehachapi Pass toward Bakersfield, Oakland, and the San Francisco Bay area. Union Pacific's Bailey Yard in North Platte, Neb., remains the largest classification yard in the world. The Pennsylvania built fly-over connections allowing opposing trains to keep moving at locations like Conway and Enola, with directional hump operations in parallel yards. New York Central planners looked at their revenues and inefficient yards following World War II and proceeded to design and construct all-new computerized hump yards at critical locations to improve velocity and reduce costs. These included Elkhart, Ind., and Selkirk, N.Y. (page 16), both of which continue to serve as hump-equipped classification yards and vital regional hubs even 70 years later in 2023.

On the prototype and on your model railroad, yards are a focal point of operations, **16**. Yards can play a supporting role or can be the focus of your modeled operations. Let's take a look at how yards work in the next chapter, beginning with terminals.

CHAPTER TWO

WATERFRONT & OTHER TERMINAL YARDS

Early railroad operations in the U.S. rapidly evolved into huge transload operations where goods arriving by sea were transferred by cranes from ships to land, repacked onto freight cars, and moved inland from the coast. Export goods flooding overseas as the nation expanded moved in reverse, with equally labor-intensive movement from freight car to land to ship, **1**. The ports of New York, Jersey City, and Baltimore in the East, New Orleans in the South, and later Tacoma, Vancouver, Oakland, and eventually Long Beach in the West, are synonymous with major rail terminals.

1 The Pennsylvania Railroad served New York Harbor via extensive carfloat operations based out of Harsimus Cove in Jersey City, N.J. This 1941 view taken from the float bridges on the eastern end of the facility illustrates the start of the line — PRR's overhead catenary systems start at the bulkhead for the floats! *Pennsylvania Railroad; collection of Ralph Heiss*

"Terminal" in both freight and passenger operations came to have a different meaning than "station" or "yard." A wterfront terminal can be a station (depot) or a yard, but it is always a defined location where the tracks end (terminate), **2**. This means terminals are necessarily stub-ended, whether at a bumper, a track on a pier, or a track that ends at a car float dock. All rail movements move between the land side and the harbor, so there are two traffic directions through each side of the facility. The track arrangements at large terminals are a complex series of switches and yard ladders to allow multiple locomotives to simultaneously work classifying cars and to allow multiple inbound and outbound trains to access tracks.

Ancillary to yard operations are the support operations, locations where cars are inspected, cleaned, repaired, and readied for their next trips. East Coast harbors were among the first, but far from the only examples. Given the congestion along tight waterfront space, railroads often moved support functions not laterally along the waterway but instead inland from the terminal itself (see "Isolated terminals" on page 24).

MODERN TERMINALS

Modern railroads have expanded the use of the terminal concept to describe some of their "hub-and-spoke" operations in the 21st century. Yards where massive volumes of intermodal (container and piggyback) traffic is originated or terminated for delivery to other nearby yards are designated terminals by today's Class I railroads, **3**. The big six North American railroads move huge volumes of freight between these origins and destinations, with much of it traveling in dedicated intermodal trains and some in manifest freights.

Today's terminal districts include all operations within a set area along each line entering the facilities and operated under a common plan. These include not just coastal areas but also inland areas such as Kansas City, Atlanta, and Denver, **4,** and smaller hubs like Harrisburg, Pa., as well. Freight is gathered from local industries and from incoming trains, classified, and assembled into outbound trains headed for another terminal; inbound traffic is classified for local delivery, **5, 6, 7**. These modern examples use smaller lines to reach customers beyond the terminal limits and allow outbound trains to be more efficient by making point-to-point trips without diversions.

An incredible version of terminal operations is apparent in looking at aerial photos from the 1950s of the area around New York Harbor. A nearly unbroken string of rail terminals existed all along the Hudson River on the coast of New Jersey. From north to south, almost 11 miles of continuous freight and passenger terminals provided a destination and origin for thousands of freight cars and tens of thousands of passengers daily. Hundreds of ferries, tugboats, carfloats, and barges plied the waters of the Hudson River and the East River, bridging the waters to allow railroads to serve New York City — some authors have referred to the extended harbor as a belt line around New York. These operations offer us a view in how to model terminals (see "Carfloats" on page 26).

PASSENGER TERMINALS

The grand passenger terminals of the classic era still dominate the public's perception of railroading. Some of those monuments to transportation are still in operation, allowing a glimpse into a past era of operational history.

Terminals exist in all sorts of configurations. Under construction on John Bauer's Sn3 Rio Grande Southern is the tiny terminal of Mayday, where the tracks end and a balloon track once existed to turn trains on the prototype.

3 BNSF's Argentine Yard (Kansas City, Kan.) includes a large intermodal terminal. Trailers and containers on cars at left await unloading in this 1997 view; the trailers at right have been parked and are ready for loading by straddle crane. Railcar storage tracks are at far right. Jeff Wilson

Passenger-car yards — particularly car and coach yards at large passenger terminals — are where the vast majority of car-cleaning and repair infrastructure is located, **8**. Between revenue runs, not only does a passenger car need inspection and maintenance, it also requires extensive interior cleaning. From basic commuter trains to intercity day trains and luxury passenger train operations, all cars are cleaned and serviced. At small terminals this may all happen in the station tracks. But at larger terminals, entire yard tracks are devoted to handle this servicing. Passengers detrain in the station, and then the train moves back out to the yard proper where it is spotted for servicing. These areas can include inspection and storage buildings as well as pits beneath the tracks to allow workers access to brake components and running gear.

A key is that all switching, cleaning, and servicing of passenger equipment

4 Today's railroading has increased use of the "terminal" idea to include operations in major inland hubs. Denver, Colo., is managed as a terminal with cooperative trackage among several railroads. And like any terminal, there's a lot to see — such as BNSF power still carrying the Santa Fe banner in 2023!

is manual: there's no automated hump yard to speed up the tasks, **9** — passenger operations are labor intensive!

In addition, many cars in passenger service require their own special services. Diners and other food-service cars have to be not only cleaned but also re-stocked and have their crews changed. Pullman cars had their own Pullman Company cleaning services and new crews. Express and baggage cars at larger terminals were routed to their own facilities (post office or Railway Express Agency) for unloading and loading. Railway Post Office (RPO) cars had their own security and handling requirements including non-railroad personnel. Further, most large passenger terminals included a car wash rack to ensure the exterior of the passenger equipment (especially windows!) was clean at the start of its run. (See "Hoboken Terminal" on page 30.)

Mechanical crews are on duty at terminals, available to make minor repairs on site (or to decide when a larger repair requires a car to be moved to another shop facility). Spare cars may replace a car set out for repair on occasion. Once a set of equipment is ready and passes inspection, it is switched back to the appropriate station track for loading.

The scale and intensity of this switching and cleaning results in a great deal of intense operations in passenger station and terminal areas and helps differentiate passenger yards from freight yards. All of these create opportunities for your model railroad and its yards.

The next pages illustrate terminal, waterfront, and carfloat operations. The chapters that follow will help you understand what prototype yards do, what your modeled yards can and should accomplish, and how to build them.

5 Short lines also use the "terminal" designation for areas central to their operations. RJ Corman Lines in Pennsylvania handles operations on a large number of former Conrail lines built originally by the Pennsylvania and New York Central. An RJC-2 crew works the yard at Clearfield, Pa., on a frigid January 3, 2009.

6 RJ Corman's system interchanges with Norfolk Southern at several locations. Cresson, Pa., on the former PRR main line is a common spot for coal and corn trains to be interchanged between the two railroads. Another RJC-2 crew handles loaded covered hoppers on a snowless February 22, 2020.

8 Passenger operations also use extensive areas of terminal districts. Coach yards like these at the Spadina Avenue terminal in Toronto, Ontario, on August 14, 1979, have many tracks, left, where coaches, diners, and sleepers are maintained between runs.
Rich Taylor

7 Shortline operations today often terminate at a connection to a Class I railroad. Trains bound for Clearfield are interchanged at Yard 5 in Cresson, essentially a long yard lead for Cresson Yard. On a sparkling July 30, 2022, Corman helper engines tack on the front of more corn loads and prepare for the up-and-down trip to Clearfield through the Pennsylvania mountains.

9 With passenger operations, crews work manually to turn locomotives and cars after trains arrive to reorganize equipment for outbound runs. At the massive St. Louis Union Station terminal, back-to-back Baltimore & Ohio E units move past the tower on April 23, 1965 while Wabash and PRR trains rest in the background.
Rich Taylor

ISOLATED TERMINAL OPERATIONS

// By Ralph Heiss

In large harbor locations such as San Francisco, Baltimore, and New Orleans, there once resided small self-contained railroad operations to serve the complicated networks of yards and carfloat operations. These properties were either physically separated from the parent railroad or only accessible by a car float connection. Some of these in fact were not owned by a Class I railroad, but by a small terminal railroad (usually owned by a group of larger area railroads) or privately owned by a warehousing company or a large industrial concern such as a steel mill or sugar refinery. Across the nation, these unique operations worked to connect isolated locations to the North American rail network.

As examples, the San Francisco docks were accessible from the Santa Fe's Alice Street Yard in Oakland via car float and the State Belt Railroad, which was owned by the City of San Francisco. The Canton Railroad in Baltimore existed to serve Bethlehem Steel's Sparrow's Point Mill. New Orleans Public Belt connected several railroads after its creation in 1908, and car floats were a huge part of its operations until the construction of the Huey P. Long bridge over the Mississippi River in 1938. These three self-contained operations flourished without physical connections to Class I railroads.

New York City had perhaps the best-known series of isolated railroad operations. This unique port, centered around one of the finest natural harbors in the world, has its eastern side in New York State and its western side in neighboring New Jersey. The only railroads that had direct access to Manhattan were the New York Central, New Haven, and Long Island Rail Road, which all operated east of the Hudson River. All other railroads coming from the west — including the Pennsylvania Railroad — were forced to terminate at the water's edge in New Jersey or in Staten Island. The unique geology and configuration of the harbor prevented bridges or tunnels from spanning the Hudson River, and until the Poughkeepsie Bridge was built in 1889 about 80 miles north of Manhattan Island, there was no way to move freight cars across the Hudson River south of Albany other than by car float.

Carfloating operations around New York Harbor

This view, taken from the float bridges at the PRR's Harsimus Cove Yard in Jersey City, illustrates the hemmed-in nature of most harbor-side yards by the 1940s, with the need for using all available space for car storage and switching. Interconnected yards allowed crews to work between floats as needed.
Collection of Ralph Heiss

began in 1866 with the Central of New Jersey, which moved its cars across to Manhattan from Jersey City. The CNJ and each of the many railroads coming from the west built small, isolated yards and warehouses within one of New York's five boroughs, and the only way to move freight there was via a carfloat connection. Railroads maintained small yards around the harbor and served them with a large marine fleet of railroad-owned tugboats, floats, and barges.

A variety of terminal operations were built and maintained by larger railroads. In some cases these isolated yard operations were located adjacent to one another, separated only by a city block. Most did not connect to any other railroad except by float. The Harlem Transfer Company opened in 1898 as a small operation in the Mott Haven section of the Bronx. This small railroad was initially owned, built, and operated by the Erie. It also had agreements in place to interchange with the Delaware, Lackawanna & Western, CNJ, and Baltimore & Ohio, each of which were desperately seeking addional capacity and building their own operations elsewhere around the harbor. The Harlem Transfer would come under the sole ownership of the DL&W in 1906, but it would maintain and operate the terminal under the Harlem Transfer Company name until successor Erie Lackawanna finally closed it in 1968. While it served a building materials company, a coal distributor, and a flour distributor on site, it was most famous for the oval-shaped freight house and circular track layout to serve it. This made for fascinating and compact trackwork to handle the influx of cars for the different railroads.

In addition, there were at least four major privately owned warehousing/industrial concerns that built and operated their own railroads and marine fleets to serve themselves and interchange with inbound railroads. The Jay Street Connecting Railroad, for example, existed to move coffee and the Brooklyn East District Terminal moved sugar. However, these railroads grew to serve as interchange partners for other railroads to access their territory. The first private terminal operation located in New York proper was the Palmer's Dock Corporation in the Williamsport section of Brooklyn in 1876. Later this operation became known as the Brooklyn East District Terminal Railroad (BEDT) after a 1906 reorganization. The BEDT was a warehousing, manufacturing, river navigation, and railroad company, and was formed to open Brooklyn to the national transportation network. Initially the small railroad was built to serve the American Sugar Co. (Domino brand) and a large cooperage factory, which made wooden barrels — at the time a popular way to ship products, sugar being just one of them.

Like many industrial switching operations, modern cross-harbor activity is today much less common due to industrial flight, residential construction, labor costs, and the move to containers and bulk traffic. Operations fell off greatly by the 1960s and 1970s, and many yards were repurposed. Freight cars do, however, still float across the harbor on the New York New Jersey Railroad, which operates the only remaining float operation in the region — trucks move the rest.

Above: Lehigh Valley's 149th Street Bronx Terminal sat on the east side of the Harlem River and is seen here circa 1939. This yard (along with those operated by the CNJ, DL&W, and Erie elsewhere in the Bronx) were completely landlocked and only accessible by car floats from New Jersey. This was the only way the railroads that terminated on the New Jersey side of the Hudson River could gain a foothold within the boundaries of New York City. Collection of Ralph Heiss

Left: The Lehigh Valley's trailer-on-flatcar (TOFC) yard at Grand Street in Jersey City was located off of the main yard and existed to serve the waterfront piers and float bridges. Originally built to handle local traffic for a freight house and a stockyard, it was repurposed in 1954 as a TOFC yard located close to the city center and the New Jersey Turnpike as seen in the background in this 1959 view. Collection of Ralph Heiss

CARFLOAT OPERATIONS // By Mat Thompson

Wagner's Point on Paul Dolkos' HO Baltimore Harbor District Railroad is served by a Western Maryland car float. Paul scratchbuilt the float and apron (which the WM calls a transfer bridge) following prototype photos. The tug *Hawkins Point* is a Walthers kit lettered for Curtis Bay Towing. The high pilot house gives the tug captain a clear view over a loaded float. Paul Dolkos

Car floats are unpowered barges configured to carry railroad cars across water. Tugboats move these floats singularly or in pairs, usually (but not always) tightly attached alongside the tug. Because of strong currents in rivers, bays, and even in some open water, towing barges behind or "on a hawser line" is not generally ideal, as wind or current can prevent the tug from controlling the tow. Some tug or towboats have a square bow to push floats. These are used mainly on rivers to counteract currents.

Rail barges and car floats have been part of the North American railroad scene almost since there have been railroads. America's first railroad, the Baltimore & Ohio, started operations in 1830 and within the decade was crossing the Potomac River by car float between Washington, D.C., and Alexandria, Va. Material movements during the Civil War found canal barges fitted with rails, then lashed together to move cars to distant railheads in Virginia. This lessened the need to break-bulk the material ahead of long hauls in horse-drawn wagons to battlefield areas.

The geography and tight spaces of New York Harbor led to extensive use of car floats and tugs. The New York Central; Erie; New York, Ontario & Western; Baltimore & Ohio; Central of New Jersey; Lackawanna; Lehigh Valley; New Haven; Pennsylvania; and other railroads ran car floats from yards on the Jersey shoreline to float docks in the boroughs of New York City.

Other operations, such as the Bay Coast Railway on Chesapeake Bay, ran floats holding up to 25 cars between Cape Charles and Norfolk, Va., from 1885 to 2012. The only access to the C&O's Brooke Avenue Yard in Norfolk was a car float from Newport News, Va. The Erie had float operations in Chicago on the Chicago River. The Wabash and later Norfolk Southern had carfloat operations across the Detroit River between Detroit and Windsor, Ontario. Farther south, Illinois Central and Missouri Pacific car floats crossed the Mississippi River.

San Francisco Bay rail traffic included Santa Fe, Western Pacific, and Northwestern Pacific, among each other for interchange and also between isolated pocket terminals around the harbor area. Milwaukee Road car floats ran between Seattle and the timber-rich Olympic Peninsula. The Canadian Pacific used small tugs and two-track car floats in British Columbia for access to isolated lumber and mining operations. The Alaska Railroad's AquaTrain ran from 1962 to 2021, ferrying cars between Canadian National's Prince Rupert, B.C., dock and Whittier, Alaska.

Car floats are flat-decked barges with rails for transporting railroad cars. Two-, three-, and four-track floats able to carry six to 24 cars were common during the steam era. In current times, float size has increased to accommodate larger cars. While car floats are not powered, some new, large barges have small motors that assist in powering rudders to aid tugs with navigation and stability when crossing rough waters.

Float proportions tend to be four feet of length for every foot of width, for stability during loading and unloading and to offset the forces of high winds and rough seas pushing

The Walthers car float has turnout points on the apron. On his HO scale Virginia & Western, Doug Kirkpatrick built a metal frog on the float and ran the closure rails across the apron gantlet-style so he could put the turnout points on land, allowing use of a switch machine. He also used code 70 nickel-silver rail in place of the plastic code 83 rail that came with the kit. Toggle bars are visible where the apron and float are joined. The dolphins and timbers between them help the tug captain guide the float into the apron. Doug Kirkpatrick

against flat-sided barges loaded with flat-sided freight cars. Rails are held in clips welded to a float's steel deck; early wood-deck floats had rails spiked to the deck. Other deck hardware includes rail stops, hatches, bitts, bollards, and cleats for lashing floats to tugboats and mooring to docks.

The link between the float and the shore is a floating bridge called an apron. One end is secured to the land and hinged while the other end floats, so the apron deck can be leveled to a float's deck height using hydraulics, pontoons, or weights. Dolphins, which are large pilings tied together in an upright position, are located near the water side of the apron to help tugs guide a float into position. The float is then secured to the apron. The float and apron rails are aligned vertically and horizontally using toggle bars, large pins that are ratcheted into metal housings on the float and the apron. To keep the car float from pulling away from the float bridge apron, ropes and sometimes chains are used to pull the car float tightly against the apron, running from the cleats on the carfloat to a winch on the apron itself.

On the land side, outbound cars are staged in yards for loading onto barges, while inbound cars are classified for further movement. Generally speaking, a support yard for a carfloat operation needs to have enough car storage

The Walthers kit has a turnout spanning the apron and float. For better tracking on his Oregon Coast Railroad, Mat Thompson placed the turnouts on shore and ran three tracks across a shortened apron. He built the float with three of the four sections, eliminating the section with the turnout. He also substituted code 83 nickel silver rail. Mat Thompson

Spokane, Portland & Seattle SW9 No. 45 is pulling cars from the float at Ilwaco, a small, isolated logging and fishing town on the Washington coast. Some of the cars will be taken to Willbridge Yard for classification. Others may be immediately added to yard transfers in the Portland area, saving yard handling. Mat Thompson

capacity to hold the cars both going to and coming off the car float at the same time. Loaded cars are often directly spotted at nearby freight warehouses and other storage facilities. When empty, cars might be switched back to the staging yard or loaded directly on an outbound float. Space is at a premium, so some larger operations had complex trackwork like double crossovers or three-way turnouts to allow more flexibility in loading the floats.

Loading requires the float to remain as stable as possible — balance is critical! For a two- or four-track float, one or two cars are loaded on one side and then the same number are loaded on the other side. This alternating-side sequence — which balances the weight on each side of the float — continues until the float is fully loaded. On a three- or five-track float, the center track would be loaded first, then the alternating-track loading sequence would begin on the side tracks. Unloading is done in reverse order.

If a tug is tied to the float during loading, the track farthest from the tug is loaded first because the tug can use its power to help keep the float steady. A variation is spotting the final car of a string being loaded with one truck on the float and one truck on the apron and repeating that until both sides are loaded.

Moving cars on and off floats is the job of a switch engine. Most operations did not allow locomotives onto floats or aprons, so idler cars were used as a "handle" to provide the reach between the locomotive and cars on the float, keeping the locomotive on solid land. Idler cars were often flat cars or gondolas with sand added for weight, although crews sometimes used any available cars.

Sometimes, however, there was no locomotive in the yard on the opposite shore. In those cases the locomotive was carried on the float to reassemble the train on the opposite shore and continue the run, such as on the CP's Nakusp Branch in British Columbia. In New York Harbor and other similar operations such as San Francisco or Baltimore, landlocked yards that were disconnected from either the parent railroad or even completely from all other railroad connections required locomotives to be occasionally moved to and from the main terminal for maintenance or to prevent damage from vandalism when left behind at the end of the day in remote operational outposts.

Carfloating operations were at their height during the steam and transition eras. Service dwindled in the 1960s and '70s with the rise of container shipping and trucking. Railroad abandonments followed in many port areas.

Because float operations were (and are) labor intensive, labor costs had a larger effect on their operations than on the rest of the railroad. Railroads that had extensive operations and maintained large fleets of tugboats and car floats had their own marine departments to run that part of the operation, managed separately from regular railroad operations. Given the expenses (labor, maintenance), railroads actively found ways to eliminate their reliance upon carfloat operations wherever possible through the 1970s and '80s, sometimes taking longer and more circuitous routes to move cars to eliminate the expense of operating a float operation. Today, carfloat operations are very rare.

Just like prototype railroads, model railroaders' interest in car floats began in the early days of the hobby — a track plan "A New Jersey O Gauge Road" featuring a car float appeared in the March 1938 *Model Railroader*.

Modelers commonly place floats and tugs on their layouts and don't move them once in place. A few daring souls build extra floats and lift or roll the floats in and out of position manually. An advantage of this approach is the floats become "fiddle yards" for moving cars on and off the railroad, or to another "shore" as part of the same layout's operation. A variation is modelers who place floats on carts and "sail" them between shores. No matter the prototype, if there's a major waterway nearby, carfloats can be a very interesting addition to yard operations.

FLOAT LOADING INSTRUCTIONS

No engines on apron or float-
Use idler cars as handles
Maximum float capacity is 12 40-foot cars

LOAD

- Middle track first
- Load two cars left side
- Load two cars right side
- Load two cars left side
- Load two cars right side

- Unload float in reverse order

Operators on Mat Thompson's Oregon Coast use these instructions to load and unload car floats. It takes about 20 minutes to unload a car float and another 20 minutes to load one. Mat Thompson

The compact stub-end yard along the Columbia River in Vancouver, Wash., supports harbor freight operations and car movements for the nearby industries. The scene is on Mat Thompson's Oregon Coast layout. The yard's five tracks can accommodate 40 cars, more than enough capacity to keep three crews busy during operating sessions. Mat Thompson

Railroads maintained a huge fleet of company-owned tugs and barges and managed them under separate operating groups. Delaware, Lackawanna & Western tug *Netcong* holds a barge in place during loading on Jim Dalberg's HO scale DL&W layout.

HOBOKEN TERMINAL – ADAPTING TO CHANGE

// By Jack Trabachino

The most fundamentally valuable quality in the physical design of a railroad network is its ability to allow operations to be adapted to the unforeseen. New ideas, new technology, and new goals can easily overwhelm a design built too closely to a specific purpose. Not unlike the prototype, the infrastructure of a model railroad, once established, becomes fixed. Fixed in place with it are its flaws: a siding that's too short, a too-sharp curve, a grade too steep. In the modeled world, as in the prototype, it is these very compromises that imbue each railroad with its unique character.

For terminal and yard operations, the history of NJ Transit's Hoboken Terminal demonstrates this adaptability. Modern commuter operations in Hoboken trace to two watershed historic events: electrification of commuter operations on the Morris & Essex Division of the Lackawanna in the early 1930s and rerouting of the Erie's diesel commuter service from its deteriorating wooden waterfront terminal in Pavonia (Jersey City) to Hoboken Terminal beginning in late 1956. This continued through the pre-Erie Lackawanna merger period until the demolition of the Erie terminal in 1961. Through the subsequent odyssey of industry consolidation — mergers, service discontinuances, urban redevelopment, transfer of commuter operations to public ownership, and, finally, publicly financed renewal — from a train movement standpoint, little changed at Hoboken. Once established in the late 1950s, the confluence of diesel-powered trains from the north with primarily electrified trains from the west became the defining feature of how Hoboken Terminal and its adjacent yards operated through today.

Under NJ Transit, the historic implications of electrification by the Lackawanna and service consolidation with the Erie were leveraged in the form of two of the agency's crowning achievements. First was conversion of the Lackawanna electrification to AC in 1984, leading ultimately to the introduction of Midtown Direct service in 1996. This routed electric, locomotive-hauled M&E trains away from Hoboken to Penn Station in New York. Second was the completion of Secaucus Junction Station, opened in 2003, which provided riders on former Erie routes the opportunity to transfer to Penn Station trains rather than be routed to lower Manhattan via Hoboken. Both enabled a commuter system historically oriented toward Wall Street and lower Manhattan to be adapted in response to a rapidly changing commuter market that, particularly in the aftermath of 9/11, focused on employment destinations to the north and east of Penn Station.

As the popularity of the new service options led to changes in commuter ridership patterns, the balance of equipment operating into Hoboken changed with it. With more Morris & Essex customers opting for trains to Penn Station, dedication of line capacity and equipment to Midtown Direct service led to reductions in the number of electric trains operating into Hoboken from the west. A few years later, with utilization of Secaucus for access to Penn Station becoming more popular, growth in rail ridership on former Erie routes meant more (and longer) diesel-powered trains originating in far northern New Jersey or New York state. In Hoboken itself, half a century on, a rebalancing of the 1956 Erie consolidation was underway, placing new demands on train and yard operations at Hoboken.

Having first preserved and maintained electrified operations through passenger railroading's most difficult years,

Hoboken Terminal was a maze of complex trackwork, highlighted by the rows of double-slip switches. Shown are the two types of equipment from early NJ Transit days — at left, the electric MU cars used on the Morris & Essex Division former Lackawanna lines and at right the new Comet coaches used on the former Erie. In the distance is a former Lackawanna F in commuter service, and to the right of it a "new" GE U34CH. Rich Taylor

YEAR	WEST / DLW	NORTH / ERIE	DLW-New York Penn	EL LINES TOTAL
1957*	284	158	0	442
1996	204	94	0	298
2003	149	124	97	370
2006	144	147	103	394
2016	102	155	115	372
2023	97	158	116	371

Total daily train counts on former EL lines.

Hoboken Terminal would take on a critical new role supporting diesel operations. To prepare for this change, in 2005, yard space once occupied by a steam roundhouse and an MU maintenance shed were replaced with a modern facility featuring dual fuel stands, a service and inspection building, raised pit track, and nine new storage tracks. By 2006, the number of Hoboken-bound trains serving former Erie stations exceeded the number of trains serving former Lackawanna routes. The elimination of direct Hoboken off-peak service on the Morristown Line in 2007 and the addition of off-peak Pascack Valley Line service in 2008 established the service distribution that continues to operate at Hoboken in 2024.

While the success of NJT projects designed to provide better access to midtown Manhattan diverted many passengers away from Hoboken Terminal, its role in supporting systemwide operations is as significant now as at any time during its history. That it does so as a diesel-oriented facility could hardly have been foreseen even by the most renowned innovators of its heyday. It is the adaptability of Hoboken Terminal's physical footprint to the changing world around it that underpins the continuing success of these services with modern commuters.

For modelers of any era, the example that prototype railroads set for us is that the defining factor in a successful operation is the ability to change, grow and evolve — even if we cannot predict the ways in which this will occur.

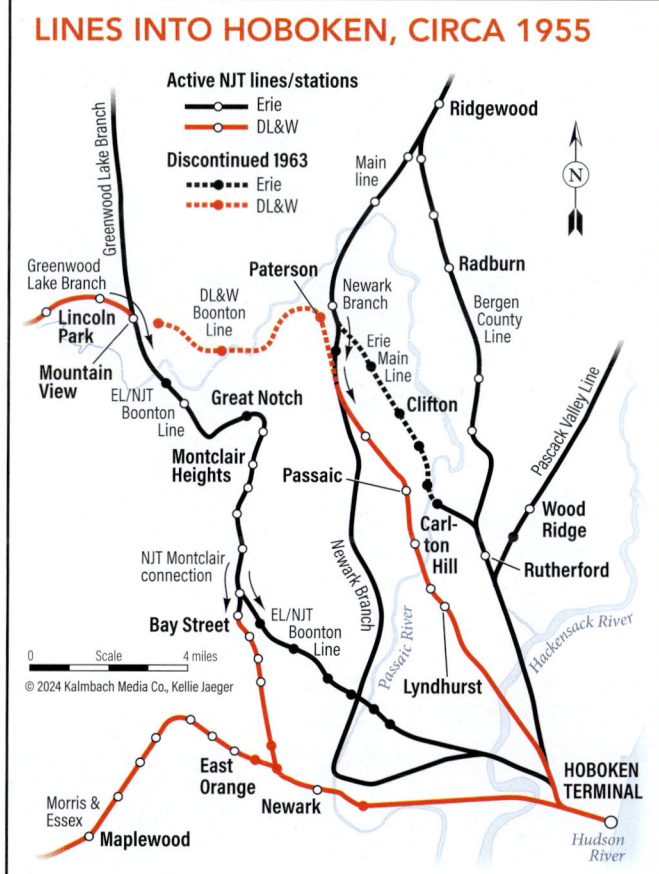

LINES INTO HOBOKEN, CIRCA 1955

Hoboken Terminal has adapted over the years to accommodate changing operations. Erie trains began to use the terminal in 1956 as passenger train use declined. The Erie Lackawanna merger made it a permanent shift. Erie Alco PA No. 860 leads a westbound passenger train on June 2, 1961. Rich Taylor

Hoboken remains a vital spot in 2023 and rush hours run fast and furious. Former CNJ GP40PH-2 No. 4101 shares the shed with Metro-North F40PH-2 No. 4914, headed to Port Jervis, N.Y., and NJT ALP45 4514 with a train headed for Hackettstown, N.J. Rich Taylor

If any locomotive signifies the constant change of Hoboken Terminal, it's the Erie Lackawanna U34CH. Passenger units financed by the government to aid EL in providing commuter service, the big U-boats lasted through Conrail and well into the NJ Transit era. April 9, 1971, finds No. 3361 sharing space with older EL power under the watchful eye of the Empire State Building across the Hudson River in Manhattan.

CHAPTER THREE

CLASSIFICATION YARDS

It's hard to imagine anything as visually impressive in railroading as a classification yard, **1**. For many industry insiders and observers, the classification yard is what we picture when we hear the word "yard." The biggest ones are the stuff of legend and are immediately recognizable by name in railroading: Santa Fe's (later BNSF's) yard in Barstow, Calif.; Belt Railway of Chicago's Clearing Yard in Chicago (along with Proviso and Cicero yards in the same city); Union Pacific's sprawling Bailey Yard in North Platte, Neb., **2**; and Pennsylvania's immense yard at Enola, **3**, immediately come to mind.

1 Classification yards are complex and fascinating. Although all perform the same basic tasks of sorting cars, each is unique regarding specific design, arrangement, and size. The Union Railroad's Duquesne, Pa., yard has been dedicated to the steel industry since it was built.

Union Pacific maintenance workers adjust the pneumatic retarder systems on the hump at Bailey Yard in North Platte, Nebraska. Beyond the hump the classification bowls spread out across hundreds of acres in the distance. This is the largest classification yard in the world. Matt Van Hattem

Others include the former Southern Pacific yards at Stockton and Roseville in California; Norfolk Southern's (former Southern Ry.) Inman Yard in Atlanta, Ga.; Oak Island in Newark, N.J., on Conrail; and — as lasting testimony to Al Perlman's brilliance — the former New York Central yards at Selkirk, N.Y., and Elkhart, Ind. The names go on. With hundreds of tracks holding and processing thousands of cars daily, and often extending more than a mile in length, each of these facilities dominates the senses in person and hold the attention of railroaders, railfans, and modelers.

Car classification is what a railroad needs to efficiently move cars from origin to customer. Doing this for thousands of cars and customers simultaneously is a work of logistical and operational art, a choreographed dance railroads call "car forwarding" — the process of moving and classifying cars efficiently while minimizing cost and maximizing safety. But what exactly is "classification"? CSX's corporate dictionary defines it as the "sorting and assembling of railway cars in station or delivery order for making up or breaking up trains or yard cuts. Cars are sorted and assembled by their destination." Said another way, classification in this sense is switching cars on yard tracks to sort them into new blocks of cars by destination, **4**.

On a warm, rainy summer night around 1970, Penn Central's former Pennsy yard at Enola, Pa., continues to work. Yard leads in the foreground will soon again host switchers assembling trains, and former Pennsylvania class N8 caboose No. 23261 at left will soon be on an outbound train across the huge PC network. Barry Trogu

All yards classify cars to some degree. In fact, anything that is dropped off or picked up at a yard is done so for a purpose: routing, interchange, or delivery.

At the peak of railroading in the U. S. — from the 1910s through the 1950s — most freight car movements were single-car lots, **5**. Small groups of cars ("blocks") meant that as late as 1975 railroads maintained humps at more than 150 operating classification yards in North America. By 2012, however, the count was down to 59 active hump yards, and that number has fallen to less than 40 in 2023. The reasons for this decline are many, and

Smaller yards make due without hump operations, such as the former Delaware, Lackawanna & Western yard at Conklin, N.Y., south of Binghamton. Abandoned under Conrail, it was reactivated by the Delaware & Hudson in the 1980s. Al Tillotson

Boxcars roll slowly behind track maintenance workers on the Boston & Maine in Bangor, Maine, on July 9, 1992. Cars like this traveled singly or in small groups from plant to customer and needed regular classification. Al Tillotson

CONRAIL'S SELKIRK YARD

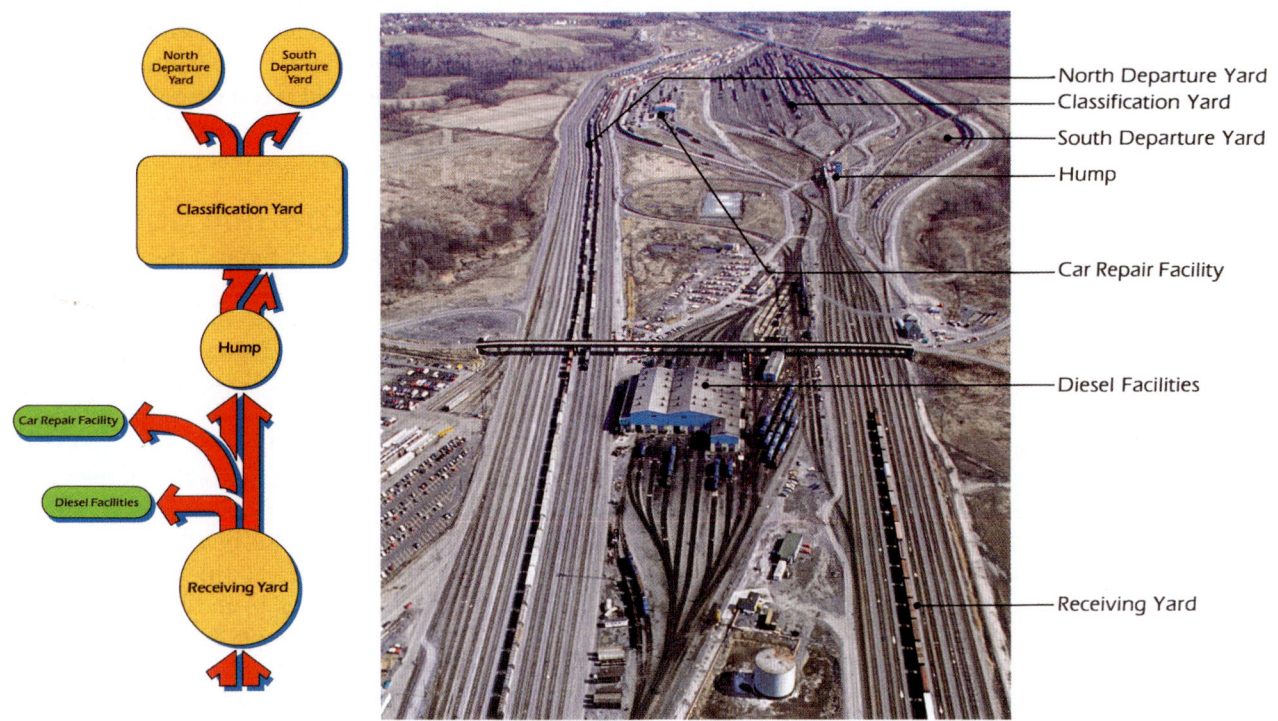

6 Hump yards vary in specific track layout, size, and traffic sources, but generally follow the same flow. The former Conrail hump yard at Selkirk, N.Y., alive and well under CSX ownership in 2023, includes the same components as other hump yards across the continent. Conrail

touch on some of the major themes of railroading over the same time. Mergers and consolidations are a big reason as is new technology for shipping freight. One of the most significant, however, is a major shift in traffic from carload traffic to intermodal traffic — from boxcars to containers — and unit trains.

COMPONENTS OF A CLASSIFICATION YARD

No two yards are identical, but nearly every classification yard contains the same or similar components with specific purposes and design features, and cars are handled in similar fashion.

"Loose-car railroading" — a term we hear often now in the railroad media and in online forums and resources — describes the traditional process of moving a car or group of cars from origin to destination. Some

7 David Olesen models CSX in the mid 1980s on the former Chesapeake & Ohio, and he represents Ronceverte, W.Va., and its small yard on his railroad. Here the Allegheny Local East diverges into the yard (left) to spot individual boxcars and covered hoppers for local customers as a westbound manifest passes.

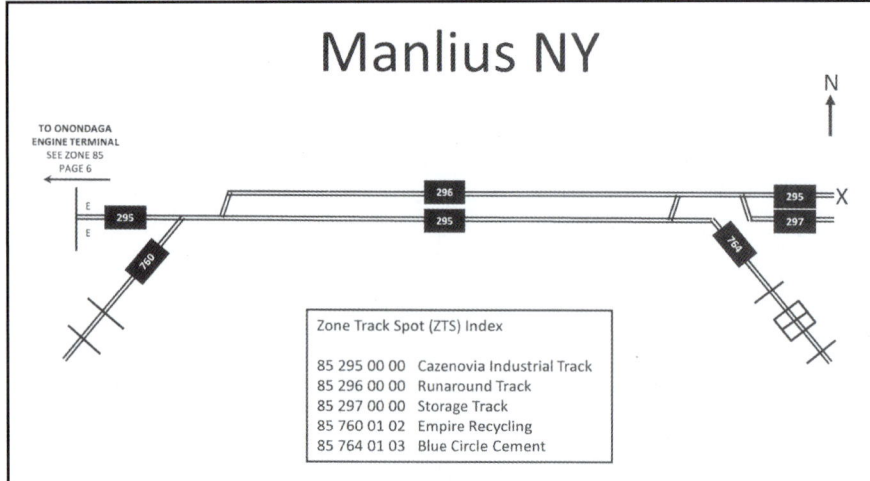

8 Conrail management, working with crews and customer service teams, developed an extensive system of "Zone-Track-Spot" maps for each division. In fact, every car spot on the system had a specific name, with specific spots for cars. Crews carried the ZTS maps with them and customers could dictate specific spots for inbound cars. This is the ZTS map for Manlius, N.Y., where our gondola was picked up from Empire Recycling.

customers may receive a car a month, others get a dozen or more daily. With cars from a variety of customers needing attention, each car is collected, then sorted by destination.

The photo and diagram in **6** show the many components of a classification yard, using Conrail's Selkirk Yard (Albany, N.Y.) as an example. Specific features vary among yards, but the illustration and flow chart show the progression of operations. Trains arrive and are placed in a track in the receiving yard. Road diesels go to the ancillary shop facilities for refueling and maintenance; any cars needing repairs go to a neighboring car repair facility. Cars are pulled from receiving tracks and sorted — in Selkirk's case, over a hump; other yards are flat-ground switched. Once cars are classified, a switcher pulls them from the classification tracks and takes them to outbound departure tracks (Selkirk has separate departure yards for north- and southbound trains). Road power is then added (cabooses would be added as well prior to the 1970s; end-of-train devices since then).

FOLLOW THAT GONDOLA

Let's walk through the process of a car or group of cars arriving at a classification yard. We will use Conrail's former New York Central DeWitt Yard (near Syracuse, N.Y.) to show how a yard handles the car. We'll follow a gondola, CR 598600 — a 65-foot, 100-ton mill gondola — on its journey. Empire Recycling is a Conrail consignee outside Syracuse, N.Y., and is a customer that contracts with Conrail to move scrap metal to and from their siding. In our example, CR 598600 has been loaded with scrap steel at Empire; the steel was sold to Crucible Metals Corporation, a custom metal alloy foundry. Crucible is also a Conrail customer but needs the load moved to a plant located about 600 miles to the west of Selkirk, near Columbus, Ohio.

Empire is a small business and has a worker who functions as the traffic manager, who has a contact at Conrail.

9 Scale tracks make great models, too. Bill Darnaby included a scale track at East Yard on his HO Maumee Route layout. Bill Darnaby

When Empire's traffic manager calls Conrail, he advises the railroad that he has one car loaded and ready for shipment. Conrail takes the data down and adds CR 598600 to the work list for the next day's WADE-10, the local freight that works customers on that stretch of railroad. WADE-10 is the railroad's name for the train — it stands for **Wa**yfreight; **A**lbany Division, **DE**witt Yard origin, with the "10" representing a job number for crew identification.

WADE-10 goes on duty the following morning and receives a list of paperwork that shows the day's customer placements and pickups, **7**. The conductor and engineer spend a few minutes coming up with the plan for the day, then sort the train into an order conducive to the work before contacting the dispatcher for permission onto the main line to start work. CR 598600 is on their list for pickup.

Crews know these locations through customer-service orders, which include specific locations on Conrail — the

10 **With their work completed and blocks picked up at East Deerfield, Mass., on the former Boston & Maine, Guilford locomotives at right pull west into the setting sun, passing the local switch engine on the yard lead.** Al Tillotson

11 **Norfolk Southern train C42, a local working on the Pittsburgh Line, classifies cars at Tyrone, Pa., on August 11, 2017.**

CSX power idles next to the yard office on John McGuire's HO scale layout. Modern railroads may have fewer hump yards, but classification is still needed — and progresses around the clock. Auxiliary lighting makes such miniature scenes more realistic, and adding this detail is easier now than ever before. John McGuire

railroad is divided into Divisions, then Zones, Tracks, and car-by-car spots. Crews call these "ZTS" maps (usually pronounced, like many railroad acronyms, by how it sounds: "zits maps"), **8**. When the train arrives at Empire, the conductor opens the switch and directs the engineer to back into the spur to make the pickup and then add the loaded gondola to the train. After finishing the work at all customers for the day, WADE-10 chugs back to Dewitt where it sets out our gondola and all the other cars it picked up in the receiving yard.

That evening one of the yard switcher jobs — YADE-14 in our example — comes on duty; part of its work is classifying inbounds from the receiving yard. On entering the receiving yard, each car had its data scanned into the yard computers. From all that data, a clerk creates a switch list for YADE-14 showing where each car is headed. The yard crew places each car onto a different track, adding it to other cars going the same point. This can be done using a hump if the yard is so equipped or can be accomplished by using a locomotive to spot each car into specific tracks. Our car, CR 598600, is sorted with a group of cars headed westward to Columbus, Ohio (Columbus is the location of another yard that has a wayfreight that works our gon's destination, Crucible). Most yards have a scale track, either built into the hump or separately, where cars are weighed to ensure accurate billing and reporting of tonnage for train makeup. Depending on the particulars of Conrail's contract with Empire, the yard crew may need to run CR 598600 over a scale to get an accurate weight for the shipment, **9**.

The group of cars bound for Columbus is what Conrail and most other railroads refer to as a "block" — a group of cars with a common destination. The block is coupled together and moved to the departure yard. There the entire block is inspected by employees to ensure no mechanical issues exist. Minor problems are repaired in place; anything major is referred to the car shop, which requires a separate switch crew. Provided all is well, the block is cleared for pickup and the cars added to the "manifest" — the paper switch list of different blocks and different cars within the blocks — of a mainline road freight, **10**.

An outbound train can comprise several blocks of cars heading to multiple destinations; CR 598600 and its block are part of a train ultimately bound for Elkhart, Ind. The Elkhart-bound train will set out the Columbus block at Buffalo, N.Y., where it will be attached to a different train headed for Buckeye Yard, a former Pennsylvania Railroad yard in Columbus.

Upon arrival at Buckeye, the block — together with other Columbus-bound cars from other blocks — will again be routed into the receiving yard, then classified. Our gondola is switched onto a track with other cars destined for local delivery; as the day progresses and additional inbound trains are classified, other cars are added to the track. In the evening, a switch crew pulls the assembled cars from the track to a departure track. The next morning, a road locomotive is added and the resulting way freight heads out and among its other work delivers our gondola to the siding at Crucible.

After Crucible unloads the scrap metal, the cycle repeats: Crucible calls Conrail to pick up now-empty CR 598600, the railroad picks up the car and brings it to Columbus. An agent can then assign it a new load to be picked up; the car will then be classified to a new outbound block with the new destination and sent on its way.

This process, which is repeated thousands of times a day across the rail network, illustrates the central role that classification plays for freight railroads, **11**. When all freight was handled in loose car lots, dozens of classification yards were needed. Increasing use of intermodal shipping — truck trailers or containers on flat cars or well cars as opposed to traditional boxcars — as well as unit-train operations (where an entire train travels under a single waybill) has lessened the need for traditional loose-car classification.

Further, in North America, Class I railroad mileage has now been merged into just six gigantic companies, which has dramatically reduced the need for loose-car classifications, **12**. Dozens of major classification yards have been mothballed, taken out of service, or had their humps removed in the last two decades. However, many remaining major U.S. and Canadian hump yards have become truly gigantic operations, handling thousands of cars a day around the clock. You've heard the show-business term "The show must go on" — well, it's true in railroading as well: operations must continue nonstop to keep the network fluid, regardless of operational problems and challenges, **13**. (See "Anatomy of a small Class I yard" on page 40.)

And, yet, while car classification remains a central operation for today's freight railroads, the importance of the classification yard has been the topic of considerable debate. Yards are operational centers but as such are also centers of tremendous physical plant and labor costs — an especially expensive part of railroading. With the industry's shift toward longer trains and less interim classification, many formerly important classification yards have been downsized in favor of consolidating operations at other yards. Some have been repurposed.

How railroads deal with this challenge — keeping cars moving while minimizing terminal and switching times — is a topic for our next chapter.

13 The long and well-spaced nature of Tony Koester's Frankfort Yard enables his yard crews to work efficiently to keep the yard moving. The scene is on his HO Nickel Plate Road layout.
Tony Koester

ANATOMY OF A SMALL CLASS I YARD: EVOLUTION OF DENVER & RIO GRANDE WESTERN'S GRAND JUNCTION YARD

// By Mark W. Hemphill

The Rio Grande yard at Grand Junction, Colo., illustrates the evolution of a small Class I railway's yard as traffic, technology, and the economy changed from the 1800s through today. The yard dates to 1882, when it was constructed as the interchange yard between two independent but cooperative narrow gauge mainline railways, the Denver & Rio Grande, which operated 424 miles of main line from Denver to Grand Junction via Pueblo, Salida, and Gunnison, Colo., and the Denver & Rio Grande Western, which operated 346 miles of main line from Ogden and Salt Lake City, Utah, to Grand Junction.

The original yard was very simple. It added and subtracted cars from trains to match the tonnage rating of an engine and changed engines and cabooses among the trains exchanged between the two railroads. The yard consisted of three through tracks, a through house track which passed behind the depot on the opposite side of the main line (and was of the same length as the yard tracks), and an 11-stall roundhouse, with spurs to a machine shop and a storage track. Local freight delivery was made at the depot and its associated house track. Mainline meets were made through one of the three yard tracks. There was no need to block or arrange cars at this yard: Freight traffic was entirely local to the two railways — all traffic originated, terminated, or both on one or other of the lines. Hauls were short distance on the two roads, averaging less than 150 miles.

In 1890, the two roads (the Utah company renamed as the Rio Grande Western) standard-gauged their main lines. The D&RG then relocated to

enter Grand Junction from the east instead of the southeast on a new main line that crossed the Continental Divide at Tennessee Pass, replacing the original narrow gauge line crossing the Continental Divide at Marshall Pass. From Newcastle to Grand Junction, the D&RG's new line was joint trackage with the Colorado Midland Railway and was operated as the Rio Grande Junction Railway, a subsidiary of both roads. That gave Grand Junction three railway companies instead of two.

There was very little expansion required for the yard, as local business was still minimal and main-line traffic remained almost entirely local. A two-story wood-framed Union Depot was constructed, the prior depot becoming a freight house, and in 1906 a stone-veneered, masonry Union Depot replaced the prior wood affair. The yard was expanded hardly at all, gaining a fourth track, and the first industry spur appeared, serving a flour mill just east of the wye to the narrow gauge main line to Gunnison. The yard remained three-rail until 1906.

During the early decades of the 1900s, the yard was gradually expanded as local traffic grew. Until the mid-1920s, there was very little through freight business to switch or block at Grand Junction; almost all of what was received from connections at Ogden, Salt Lake, Denver, and Pueblo still terminated online. Trains dropped stock cars at Grand Junction to be loaded with livestock and refrigerator cars and boxcars for the growing agricultural production of the surrounding Grand Valley — principally apples, peaches, potatoes, oats, and wheat — and carloads of eastern merchandise. A large icehouse was constructed inside the wye, along the main track, to handle perishable loads originating at Grand Junction and surrounding stations. In the autumn harvest, loadings could exceed 100 cars daily.

Between 1925 and 1929, the Rio Grande drastically modernized its main line, facilities, and rolling stock to enable it to handle overhead traffic. This modernization stemmed from a 1920 decision of the U.S. Congress to grant the Interstate Commerce Commission the power to set minimum rates, reasoning that this change would protect small and inefficient railways like the Rio Grande from eventual abandonment. The minimum rates, which were based on the least rate a road like the Rio Grande could charge and just earn a return on investment, required the competing Union Pacific and Santa Fe to increase their rates and compete only on service. The modernization, largely completed by 1929, meant that a shipper paid the same rate whether its carload was shipped via the Rio Grande, Union Pacific, or Santa Fe, and perishables, lumber, and other traffic began finding its way to the Rio Grande.

By that time, Grand Junction Yard had grown incrementally to 16 classification tracks, but most of the yard's function was simply car storage: livestock cars idle between the spring and fall movement of sheep and cattle to and from summer range and coal gondolas with little use during the summer months when there was no demand for coal for home heating. As Grand Junction grew from a frontier town to a small city of 20,000 population, industry spurs were added piecemeal to serve a sugar factory, canneries, fruit packing houses, lumber yards, coal yards, oil dealers, and wholesalers. A stockyard just west of Grand Junction, at a location called Durham, became one of the larger cattle sale yards on the railway.

With increased passenger traffic, the main track was doubled through the yard and three through platform tracks were added. These were dual purpose, holding layover baggage cars, RPOs, and coaches that were set out and picked up at Grand Junction. The locomotive machine shop was also expanded by this time to become the third largest on the system after Burnham Shops in Denver and Salt Lake City Shops.

Grand Junction's engine-change function continued — the ruling grades to the east and west of Grand Junction differ sufficiently to encourage that practice. To the west, to Helper (the foot of the helper grade to Soldier Summit), the ruling grades were 1.1% in each direction. To the east, the railway rose steadily to Minturn, the helper terminal at the foot of Tennessee Pass, on a ruling grade of 1.38%. Rio Grande practice in the steam era was to load all trains to the limit of the locomotive, accepting an over-the-road speed of 10 to 15 mph with dead freight and 15 to 20 mph with symbol freight. Because of the engines used on either side of Grand Junction, tonnage reductions were made in each direction as required, with extra trains called once sufficient tonnage had accumulated. The yard's primary functions remained setout and pickup of tonnage-reduction cars, switching of local industry cars, and car storage.

Generally, Grand Junction cars would arrive in a block at either the head end or rear end of trains, having been sorted by the terminals in Denver, Pueblo, and Salt Lake City to avoid any flat-switching of whole trains at Grand Junction. Salt Lake City and Pueblo both had sizeable yards so typically sent trains across the D&RGW "mine run," sorting out and blocking only the "shorts" (the

The D&RGW's company photographer in October 1978 looked west from Grand Junction's East Yard tower into the hump yard bowl. At right, a train crew walks to a 13-car eastbound local made up in a Group 1 bowl track, its caboose already coupled up. An SD9 to its right is working as a trim and hump engine. At far right, a westbound train from Pueblo, No. 71, leaves Grand Junction after a recrew — East Yard was only humping eastbound trains by that time. It has a large pickup of cement on its head end from Ideal Basic Cement at Portland, Colo. At left, a cut of hoppers loaded with coal rolls into the Group 2 bowl tracks. The empty space at left was reserved for the planned Group 3 bowl tracks, which were never needed and never built. The large buildings at far right were the warehouses of Salt Lake Hardware and Grand Wholesale, distributors of building materials and groceries in Grand Junction and western Colorado. Chuck Conway

cars destined for intermediate locations such as Grand Junction). Trains arriving at the far terminal — for example, a Pueblo train arriving at Salt Lake City — were then flat-switched to sort them into local cars and interchange cars, organized into blocks for each of the D&RGW's connecting railways and sent on their way.

The Great Depression forestalled any need for further expansion of Grand Junction's facilities. Traffic declined by 1932 to half of its 1929 peak and did not fully recover until 1939, then accelerated rapidly during World War II, in 1945 reaching six times the 1939 "normal" volume.

With the late 1934 completion of the Dotsero Cutoff, connecting the Rio Grande's Royal Gorge Route main line via Tennessee Pass, to the Denver & Salt Lake Railway's Moffat Tunnel Route line to Denver, the Rio Grande now had a new problem, which was to sort cars received from connections at Salt Lake City and Ogden into trains for Denver and Pueblo. Initially, the eastbound sorting was handled by Roper Yard in Salt Lake City, a flat-switch yard constructed in the 1920s. Westbound classification continued to be handled at Pueblo and Denver. Pueblo blocked trains received from the Missouri Pacific and transfers from the joint Santa Fe-Colorado & Southern yard. In Denver, a new flat-switch yard called North Yard (constructed in 1950) received through trains from the Burlington and Rock Island and transfers from the Union Pacific and the joint C&S-Santa Fe yard.

HUMP YARD ADDITION

As freight schedules sped up after World War II in the effort by railways to remain competitive with trucking, the overload in Roper Yard, North Yard, and Pueblo became apparent. None of those yards was really set up for production classification of trains. With Grand Junction being the nearest terminal to the west of the junction between the Moffat Tunnel and Royal Gorge routes, and since it had flat, arid, warm, and inexpensive farmland surrounding it, Grand Junction gained a new hump yard in 1953. This was East Yard, so named because it was east of the wye to the original narrow gauge main line via Gunnison. The original Grand Junction yard was renamed West Yard. East Yard as built was about three miles long, with a receiving yard of six tracks (each about 125 cars long) and a 24-track hump bowl, arranged in three groups of eight tracks, numbered 1, 2, and 4. Space was left for Group 3, to be constructed as traffic grew, though the traffic never arrived and Group 3 was never constructed. Three tracks in Group 1, the nearest to the main line, were extended to the west so they could also serve as the eastbound departure tracks. Similarly in Group 4, the farthest from the main track, the three southernmost tracks were extended to the west to serve as the westbound departure tracks. All other bowl tracks were about 30 cars long.

Ancillary facilities at East Yard included five repair tracks, five wash and cleanout tracks for freight cars, and two run-through engine fueling and servicing tracks, all constructed

Union Pacific purchased Southern Pacific and the former Rio Grande properties in 1996 and a condition of that deal was that BNSF be granted trackage rights over the former D&RGW main line. BNSF has its own crews for both road trains and locals based at Grand Junction. Here we see power for BNSF locals tied down at the yard office and station complex. *Philip A. Brahms*

along a hump bypass lead. Grand Junction performed light engine repairs and essential wheelset or traction motor/wheelset "combo" change-outs only, with heavy repairs sent to Burnham Shops in Denver. A five-story brick yard tower at the hump housed the yardmaster and clerks and, on the fourth floor, the retarder machine. Other buildings included a herder building at the top of the hump which controlled the remote-control switch machines for the tracks connecting the receiving yard to the hump, a RIP (repair-in-place) track building, a caboose and signal maintainer's servicing and stores building, and a diesel servicing tool and stores building. At some later time a single-track diesel servicing building was constructed.

The yard was laid out to leverage the general descending grade westward toward the river to aid in switching. The receiving yard was constructed on a 0.3% descending grade to the west. As it approached the hump, the hump leads rose at 0.5% to the crest. Beyond the crest, the retarder tracks initially descended at a 4.1% grade through the master retarder, then softened in steps to 2.08% for 100 feet, 1.30% for 100 feet, and 0.80% for 150 feet, the latter incorporating the secondary retarders. The classification tracks in the bowl descended at 0.20% until 300 feet from their ends, at which point they rose on a 0.40% grade to help prevent roll-outs of cars that were not sufficiently slowed by the retarders.

BUILT FOR EFFICIENCY

East Yard was designed to receive, classify, and depart trains in 1½ hours. Initially, the yard classified trains in both directions, but this was soon limited to eastbound trains only. The limitation was instituted because freight schedules coordinated with the Burlington, Rock Island, and MoPac to the east, and with the Southern Pacific and Western Pacific to the west, were designed so that the Midwestern carriers assembled through trains specifically for either the SP or the WP, thus eliminating the need for expensive and time-consuming classification on the Rio Grande.

As a result, a typical eastbound train arriving at Grand Junction was classified into Denver and Pueblo cars. The Denver cars were blocked for the Burlington, the Rock Island, and shorts and others; the Pueblo cars were blocked for the MoPac, Santa Fe/C&S, and shorts and others. The next eastbound train arriving at Grand Junction was similarly classified. Since traffic volumes via Pueblo and Denver in the 1950s were approximately equal, two inbound trains became two outbound trains, one now blocked for Denver's North Yard, the other for Pueblo's Roger Yard. If there was an imbalance, the third inbound train would fill out either the Pueblo or Denver train that hadn't left. The practice at Roper Yard in Salt Lake City was to send eastbound trains out in pairs so that as little as time as possible was lost waiting at East Yard in Grand Junction. Generally, the East Yard hump sorted cars so that each end block of an outbound train went into two short classification tracks and the middle block went into one of the long classification/departure tracks.

As soon as the train arrived in the receiving yard, the road power uncoupled and went to the service tracks. Car inspectors checked the inbound cars and bled the air reservoirs, which required about 15 to 20 minutes. While this was going on, the hump engine coupled to the east end of the train. From 1953 to 1965, the hump engine was a Fairbanks-Morse H15-44 paired with a slug built from a retired Baldwin VO-660 switch engine. After 1965, the hump engine was usually an SD9. As soon as the carmen were finished, the hump engine began processing the train over the hump. Usually the caboose on the inbound train remained attached and went over the hump. Once the last car went over the hump, the hump engine followed over the crest to trim the outbound train. It picked up the outbound train's front-end block (or blocks) from one of the short tracks, pulled it back up the hump and set it over on the middle block.

A trim engine, another H15-44, doubled over the rear blocks onto the middle block. Ground crews walked the train and coupled the air hoses. The road engines returned from the service track, coupled on and performed an air test, and the train departed.

Though westbound trains no longer passed over the hump, most had a Grand Junction setout, particularly intermodal trains from Denver such as No. 99. If carrying a setout, the train would depart North Yard with the Grand Junction cars at the rear and with two cabooses, one at the rear and one between the Grand Junction and Salt Lake cars. After the train stopped on the main line at Grand Junction for the crew change, crews would "pull the pin" between the Salt Lake caboose and the Grand Junction cars and depart. A switch engine would then pull the Grand Junction cars down to the piggyback ramp inside the mainline curve just east of the depot and adjacent to the freight house, team track, and the Rio Grande Motor Ways garage and yard.

After the construction of East Yard, West Yard declined into storage and local switching use. East Yard maintained its role of sorting eastbound manifest trains until after the 1996 merger of Rio Grande successor Southern Pacific with Union Pacific. Through manifest trains were then rerouted from the former Rio Grande to UP's main line through Wyoming, and the East Yard hump was closed. The yard continues in use as of 2023 for local traffic and to serve unit coal trains and oil trains that originate on the former Rio Grande. Many of the West Yard tracks have been removed and the remainder are used mostly for car storage.

The evolution of Grand Junction Yard shows three things: first, that yards aren't standard but are constructed and adapted to specific needs of traffic flow. Second, that yards evolve as the traffic evolves. And third, that once a pattern is established, yards repeat the pattern until the traffic changes. Nothing is random about yard operations.

CHAPTER FOUR

BLOCKING OPERATIONS

Railroading is used to major changes, **1**. In an industry as old and complex as this one, operations and equipment must change and adapt even though fundamental principles remain the same. Just as ships were once loaded and unloaded by hand, railroading for more than a century was a labor-intensive, hands-on operation that classified cars every few hundred miles, **2**.

1 CSX train Q009, a UPS hotshot bound for Chicago, kicks up the packed snow on Feb. 9, 2016. This train is bypassing Buffalo's Frontier Yard, holding Main Track 1 westbound through CP (control point) 433. By this point piggyback trailers were fast disappearing in favor of containers, a reminder that railroading is always changing.

As the world has modernized and as many tasks were automated, railroads — particularly in the 20th century — worked to minimize rapidly increasing labor costs to maintain profits. Increased wages during and after the two world wars and then deregulation in the 1980s meant nothing in railroading was taken for granted very long.

Railroads refer to groups of cars being handled as a "cut," and to a group going to the same intermediate or final destination as a "block." An intermediate destination can be a classification or division point yard (including on another railroad), and a final or ultimate destination can be a customer or consignee, **3**. As train length and speed increased in the 1920s and 30s, car classification at every major yard along a route — meaning laborious flat switching of cars back and forth — became increasingly costly and burdensome, imposing expensive delays and errors. Car velocity — an average measure of the speed of a car across a division or system — has always been dependent on dwell time; dwell time is defined as a measure of how long a car sits in a yard pending handling. Velocity was held low by having to stop cars for classification and then re-classification several times on a trip. The more stops, the more times the car was switched or classified; the more stops, the higher the cost and the slower the velocity.

As trains grew in size, railroaders figured out that cars bound for locations beyond those interim yards could be grouped together in separate blocks of cars in a train, and that every block then didn't need to be reclassified at each stop, **4**. The basic economics of blocking is inescapable: if groups of cars in a train are coupled together by

The Lehigh Valley terminal in Jersey City, N.J., was a congested and busy network of interchanges, classification yards, and labor-intensive freight transload locations. Boxcars are unloaded by hand and the freight repacked in this May 1945 view as a distant switch engine approaches to move more cars. Ralph Heiss collection

BNSF GE road power exchanges blocks of covered hoppers at the "Wash Yard" at Wellington, Utah, on Union Pacific's former Denver & Rio Grande Western. The BNSF was granted trackage rights as a condition of the UP/SP merger in 1996 and uses the rights on a daily basis.

destination, then the train can stop at fewer locations along the line for less time. Instead of setting out individual cars, road trains drop blocks for local work to be done by separate trains, leaving the road train to get moving again after just a few moves.

Within a yard, blocks increase standard work cycles, so that yard crews classify cars to the same outbound destinations on the same tracks and in the same order each day, which means faster moves, less need to communicate changes, and fewer errors.

INTERMODAL ADVANTAGE

Intermodal trains have grown from a tiny part of rail operations in the 1950s into the largest part of freight volume for many railroads. Beginning with trailers on flat cars, then containers, and eventually double-stacked contain-

Conrail train TV-24, a Chicago-Boston intermodal train, approaches DeWitt Yard in East Syracuse, N.Y., on Feb. 14, 1998. The head block of double-stack containers will be dropped at DeWitt Yard, with the piggybacks behind continuing to Boston without further classification.

ers in specialized well cars, intermodal has become a dominant traffic component, **5**.

Economics and the advent of digital tracking and logistics management have favored containerization for decades, and railroads provide the long-distance link for such movements on land. Containers are largely standardized for either international or domestic operations. Each allows freight to be moved with relative ease between ships, trains, and trucks. Blocking operations which started with miscellaneous cars were a natural fit for intermodal.

Many yards that once classified loose cars, including many former hump yards, have been altered or expanded to now handle intermodal operations. Entire new intermodal yards have been built, such as Kansas City Logistics Park (known locally as "KCLP"), a massive 3,000-acre development in Edgerton, Kan., southwest of Kansas City. The vision was for a rail-served industrial center serving not only as a yard to interchange blocks of intermodal freight for BNSF's intermodal network but also as a destination for BNSF intermodal trains on the famous "Transcon" route of the former Santa Fe.

CASE STUDY: DEWITT YARD, SYRACUSE, N.Y.

The nature of modern railroading required changes on older routes, especially in the northeastern United States where many relatively small railroads grew, combined, and downsized. One prime example is the sprawling DeWitt Yard on the New York Central main line outside Syracuse, N.Y., **6**.

What we know as the New York Central Railroad was an amalgamation of a number of shorter railroads originally built across New York State following the Hudson River north from New York City, then west at Rensselaer, N.Y., through Albany toward Utica, Syracuse, Rochester, and Buffalo — following the low-grade water level route of the Erie Canal. Cornelius Vanderbilt — who is remembered as "The Commodore" — was the sharp, ruthless, and decisive creator of the NYC. The company purchased the smaller roads along the Mohawk Valley through the 1870s and 1880s, creating a juggernaut that eventually extended down the Hudson to the tidewaters of New York Harbor, west to the Great Lakes in Buffalo, and eventually all the way to Chicago. Other railroads served the same markets, but the Water Level Route had more moderate grades, fewer curves, and was less costly to maintain.

Vanderbilt's railroad built a large classification yard just east of the industrial city of Syracuse in a small village known as DeWitt, N.Y. Named after the infrastructure visionary DeWitt Clinton, the town of DeWitt was a station along the Erie Canal. The town commemorates a man who was elected as a U.S. senator, mayor of New

Routes that long saw domination by coal or merchandise traffic are now regularly hosting intermodal trains. Norfolk Southern's former Norfolk & Western main line westward from Roanoke, Va., hosts train 21A, which at the time was running to St. Louis for interchange with Union Pacific on a cool May 27, 2017.

DeWitt Yard on CSX is a sign of the times: a yard that once classified thousands of freight cars daily that today hosts dozens of daily intermodal trains, most of which stop to drop or pick up blocks of cars. On Jan. 7, 2014, the yard is loaded with intermodal blocks that sit adjacent to the flat-switching operations beyond in the former hump yard bowl. DeWitt today is a crossroads in the intermodal network of CSX.

York City, and the seventh governor of New York, but is now primarily known as the spark behind construction of the Erie Canal. It is ironic but unsurprising that the town of DeWitt was chosen to host a massive freight yard for the Central, the railroad that became the natural successor to the canal.

Even in a changing industry, DeWitt Yard remained a key location for the railroad. The NYC rose to incredible power and then slid into bankruptcy, merged into the Penn Central, and was then swallowed by government reorganization into Conrail. The hump, long a symbol that defined important classification yards, remained in operation until the early 1990s, **7**. Dewitt's small trailer-on-flatcar terminal was originally tucked west of the yard. That DeWitt remained so critical for classification even given the sprawling and more modern Selkirk Yard just 150 miles to the east is a testimony to the original design and location of DeWitt and to the traffic density on one of the most important main lines in the Western Hemisphere.

However, time waits for no railroad. As deregulation took hold in the mid-1980s, the traditional traffic base of railroads fundamentally changed. Without government-set rates for cars between two points, railroads were free to charge shippers as each company's management dictated and traffic allowed. Railroads charge by the mile and class of goods so that, without controlled rates, a longer haul gener-

47

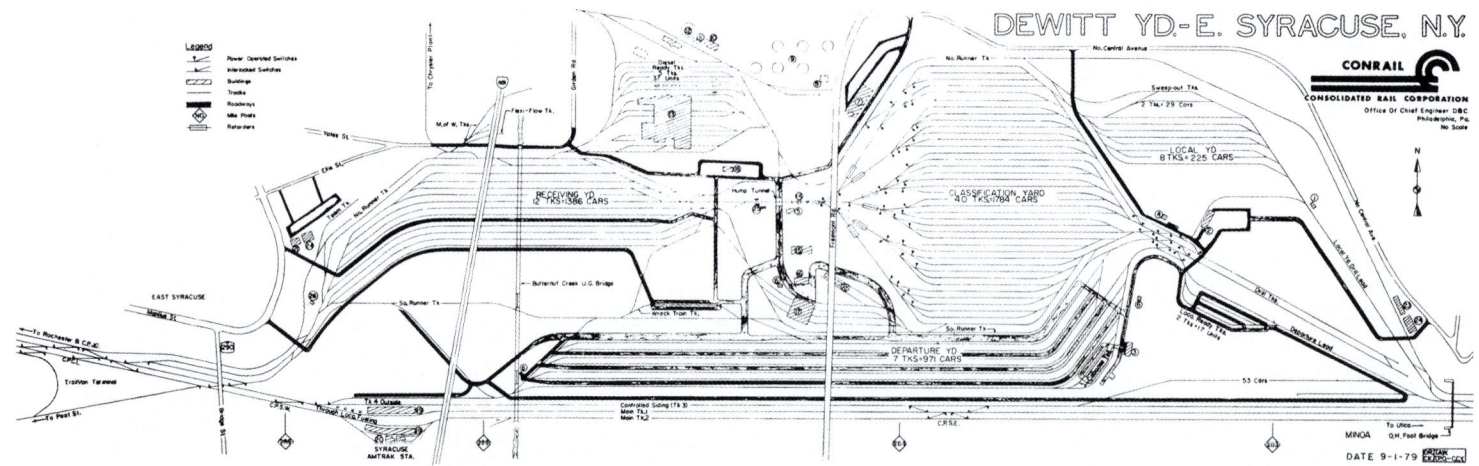

7 Conrail's schematic of Dewitt Yard in 1979 is drawn looking north from the south side and shows the hump in the center of the image. The much smaller intermodal "TrailVan" terminal is also shown at far left, west of the main yard.

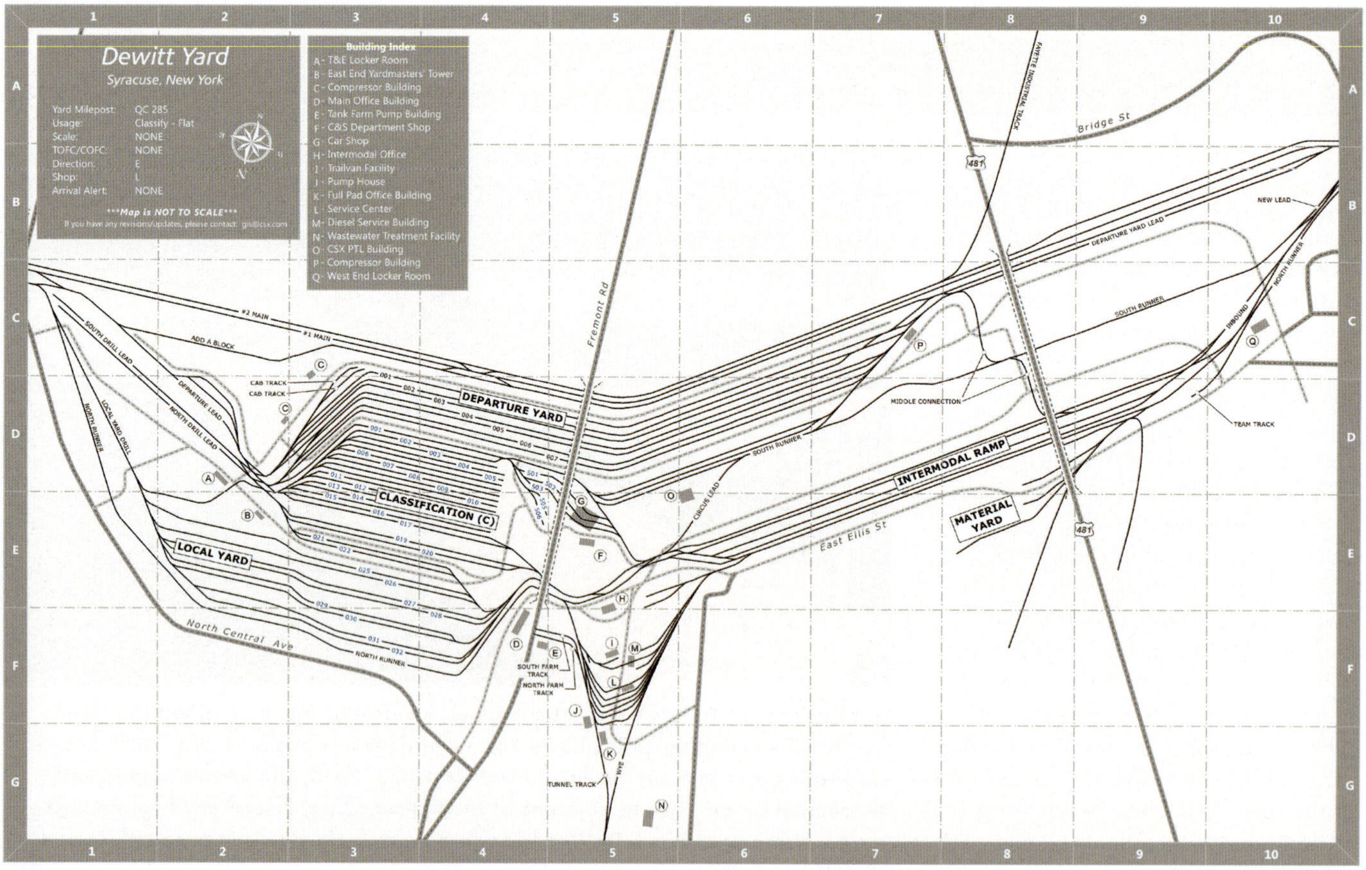

8 After acquiring half of Conrail in 1999, CSX took what CR started and continued further. CSX chose to redraw the map looking south from the north side — opposite of Conrail's map — which highlighted the new intermodal and departure yards. This version from 2022 clearly shows a facility where intermodal comes first.

Conrail train TV-80W, a UPS hotshot, comes around a curve on the Onandaga Cutoff and into CP 277 on a warm Oct. 28, 1994, with a load of dedicated UPS and U.S. Mail traffic for off-ramping in Worcester, Mass. Modeling the Chicago Line in the Conrail era means lots of intermodal trains.

ates more revenue than a shorter haul. After deregulation, railroads could for the first time in a century solicit traffic based not only on service but on the rate itself. The marketing groups could charge a premium for traffic that either was expensive to move or got in the way of more profitable traffic. Railroads, in other words, could for the first time in memory price themselves out of providing service. As a result, trains in the early 1990s began to be filled with cars traveling longer and longer distances — cars that did not need to be classified at Dewitt, **7, 8**.

At the same time, there was incredible growth in intermodal traffic on principal U.S. main lines. What this meant, with railroads able to offer and charge for premium services and an existing core of mail and parcel trains, was that the foundation was in place to revolutionize modern railroading.

In stepped the Southern Pacific in the mid-1980s with dedicated double-stack trains of import traffic that rapidly increased in number. Double-stacks are excess-height well cars that allow standard containers to be stacked two high. SP's partner for the move to the East Coast was Conrail, which after 1976 controlled three of the four main trunk lines between Chicago and New York City (the old PRR, NYC, and Erie lines). The new extra-height trains fit the extra-height clearances that had originally been built into the Erie main line (to fit the Erie's original six-foot gauge, but that's another story), and Conrail took advantage of the opportunity the extra clearances represented. However, as traffic grew, the operational reality was that the Erie had three separate summits between Buffalo and tidewater in New Jersey, while the New York Central had but one — and that one was more than 500 feet lower in elevation than any of Erie's.

Conrail decided to reinvest in the former NYC, raising clearances on the Chicago Line to create a premier intermodal artery, **9**. And DeWitt, where the hump was processing fewer and fewer cars, happened to be a prime location for an intermodal yard. With its setting just minutes from the junction of Interstates 81 and 90, Dewitt's location means that truckers off-ramping intermodal at DeWitt are able to make a one-day round trip that reaches nearly 30% of the U.S. population.

What followed was a reimagination of what DeWitt could do for the future on Conrail. Conrail decided it would consolidate hump operations at Selkirk to the east and at Buffalo to the west and consolidate intermodal operations at DeWitt. After many decades as a central feature of DeWitt yard, the hump was removed from service. While the classification bowl remains for flat-switching, the receiving yard was largely paved over to create a massive intermodal facility. Overhead cranes easily load trailers or stack containers onto flat or well cars. The old intermodal terminal west of the yard became a transload facility. No longer would mainline trains need to work the awkward access to the spur. Instead, long controlled sidings were improved in the yard proper to allow mainline trains easy access to drop or pick up blocks of cars for other trains. Running tracks were realigned to ensure entire trains could clear the main line while working DeWitt. Manifest trains too benefited from the ability to enter a running track, clear the main line and do their work dropping or picking up a block of cars.

As of 2024, CSX still uses the reimagined DeWitt as Conrail had envisioned: a true intermodal hub serving the needs of the most densely populated region in North America.

REFLECTIONS ON RAILROADING: WORKING CONRAIL'S YARDS // By Douglas Watts

Conrail's TV-13 storms west into Syracuse, N.Y., with intermodal traffic from Boston en route to Chicago. Conrail's intermodal network demanded coordination across all operating departments, as described by Doug Watts in his experiences as a young trainmaster.

Railroad freight yards are generally thought of as locations where trains arrive and cars are classified, locomotives serviced, rolling stock inspected, and new trains built and dispatched. Freight yards indeed combine the activities listed above and also include members of multiple departments working in concert to ensure customers' freight will move safely and efficiently through the terminal and on to final destinations. From my experience, teamwork was critical throughout a rewarding 26-year career spanning five different railroads.

The first in-depth focus I had was with the first railroad I worked for — Conrail — where I was employed from 1985 through 1999. I worked in and around yards of varying sizes as an assistant trainmaster in the trainmaster's training program, then as a transportation analyst on a team conducting system-wide transportation division reviews. I was promoted to trainmaster on Conrail's New Jersey Division in 1986.

During those first years on Conrail, I was assigned to visit many freight yards: Conway, Pa.; Big Four (Avon, Ind.); Elkhart, Ind.; Selkirk, N.Y.; Buckeye (Columbus, Ohio); Oak Island (Newark, N.J.); Frontier (Buffalo, N.Y.); DeWitt (Syracuse, N.Y.); and Enola, Pa. Conrail was a big railroad and moved its managers throughout the system. At each one, I would meet with members of the departments involved with operations and I was able to gain an insight into the scope of work performed.

After my promotion to trainmaster, I worked at the yards on that division: Bayway and Port Reading served the oil refineries and industries around Linden, N.J.; South Kearny, Croxton, and North Bergen yards served the north Jersey intermodal market, the big hump yard at Oak Island, and Browns Yard in Old Bridge, N.J. Each yard was different, but one constant is that it took amazing teamwork to accomplish the mission at hand — something I was able to experience up close.

SOUTH KEARNY, N.J.: TRAILVAN TERMINAL

During fall 1986 I worked second shift as trainmaster at South Kearny intermodal. The overall layout of the yard was cramped, but it was responsible for handling time-sensitive, premium intermodal trailer traffic. This included everything

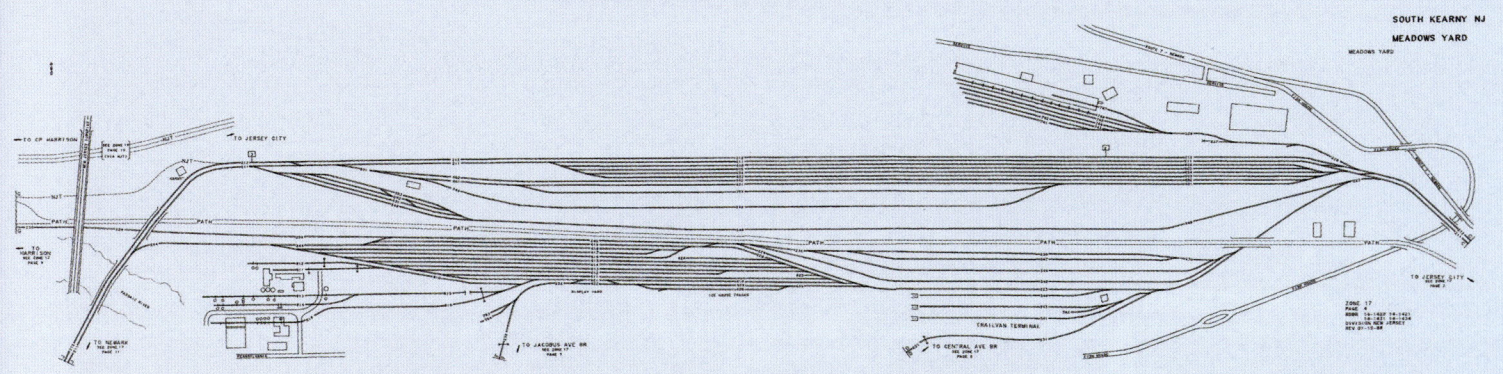

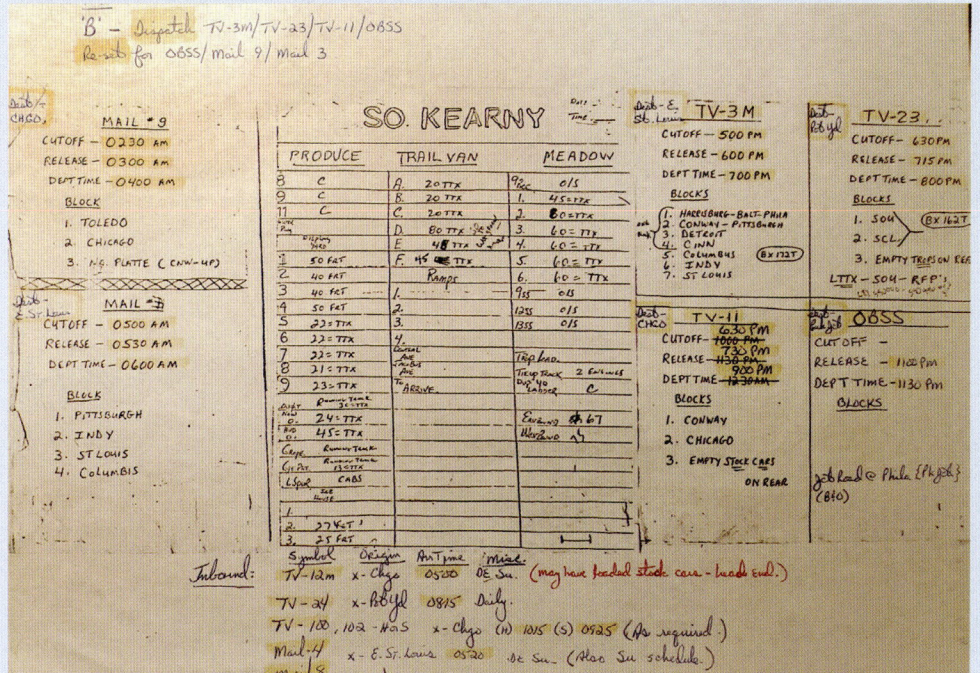

This map shows the South Kearny (N.J.) intermodal yard as it appeared in Doug's era.

This is an example of a South Kearny "cheat sheet" that Doug and other managers used to help ensure work stayed on time and that it was done in an organized manner.

that could ride a priority train: perishables, U.S. Mail, UPS, and freight-forwarder shipments. On our shift, the South Kearny team dispatched three scheduled, high-priority intermodals:

• TV-3M, destination East St. Louis, Ill.; 7:00 pm departure.
• TV-23, destination Potomac Yard, Va.; 8:00 pm departure.
• TV-11, destination Chicago, Ill.; 9:00 pm departure.

Note those times: three hot trains from one yard in just two hours! Then, once those trains were dispatched, part of the pad was reset with empty TOFC platforms (cars) for the *Orange Blossom Special*, the CSX interchange train for UPS trailers that departed at 11:30 pm bound for the South.

South Kearny is where I learned about the terms "footboard yardmaster" and "footboard trainmaster." Due to the priority of the trains and congested nature of the terminal and surrounding area, the yardmaster and I worked separately ensuring that final make-up of the three critical trains was complete. We made sure the head-end crew (conductor, engineer, and brakeman) were safely aboard, then used our assigned radios to work on the ground and assist the crew as they made their doubles to put the trains together.

Tracks A, B, and C were located on the south side of the terminal and D, E, and F were on the north side. Through the middle of the terminal was the double track PATH (Port Authority Trans Hudson) commuter operation. This may seem odd, but since South Kearny and the tracks upon which PATH runs were all former Pennsylvania Railroad property, it's a refection of today's reality in yards — lots of moving parts!

The South Kearny senior trainmaster worked the daylight shift and provided me with detailed training on the terminal layout, working with the yardmasters on timely resets for the pad tracks. The Trainmasters also had to make sure to check the east end of each track to make sure the angle cock was closed on the last car on each track. If not closed ahead of time, the air would blow through when doubling cuts of cars and delay building the train.

Teamwork between my yardmaster and I, the train crew, and the mechanical department was key to timely train departures. One night, I was responsible to assist the crew

Port Reading Yard remains a busy yard today. On April 2, 1997, three separate jobs work lines of chemical and local traffic where Reading Company coal trains once were emptied onto barges.

in putting together the blocks of TV-11. Radio procedure when talking with the head end on car lengths to couple up multiple tracks was paramount. Here I was, talking a crew down to the couple and I couldn't see them! The radio was the lifeline. Another night, on a two-track double, the lead car of the second cut was on a slight curve and I wasn't able to move the couplers. Then the car department rolled up and said, "we have you." They reminded me that whenever I needed help, I shouldn't hesitate to call them. I always appreciated that camaraderie and always made sure to be with them when TV-11's marker was hung and the brake test was performed.

It wasn't always pleasant. During fall 1986 a small volume of livestock still moved by rail. Loads rode the head end of TV-12 from Chicago and empty cars rode the hind end of TV-11 back west. Since they were on TV-11, they were ours to handle. One night I had to help hang the marker on an empty 86-foot stock car on the rear of the train. When the wind shifted, the stench was unbearable!

Teamwork between members of the departments noted above was crucial to our ability to consistently dispatch the premium service trains for which we were responsible on time. And "on time" at that point in Conrail history meant no later than *one* hour after scheduled arrival time. Imagine that in 2024 railroading! And the consequences were dire — if the train was "late" per this commitment, then the entire movement was zero revenue to Conrail.

BROWNS YARD, OLD BRIDGE, N.J.

Following working at the Oak Island hump yard in Newark, N.J., winter 1986 to the spring 1987, I was re-assigned to the industrial territory covered by Browns Yard just to the south, in Old Bridge, N.J., from spring 1987 through the summer of 1988.

This location was quite different from working on the northern end of the terminal territory. Browns was significantly smaller than Oak Island and didn't have the "rush" of South Kearny TrailVans, but still served a customer base that generated $10 million in revenue in 1987-1988. I was responsible for six crews comprising three yard jobs and three local jobs. One yard crew built the three locals and the two remaining yard crews traveled out to serve multiple customers. I rode with my crews and talked with them about their work, and learned the territory and about our customers.

In a smaller yard, I was more involved with more groups than up at South Kearny. Maintenance of way handled track, signal, and bridge issues that came up. And of course the power bureau and dispatchers worked to manage movement of locomotives and trains.

My daily inbound train was YJOI-60 (Yard job, Jersey Division, Oak Island start) from Oak Island. It delivered cars down the Chemical Coast Secondary including Port Reading Yard, then ran via New Jersey Transit (NJT) across the Raritan River, rejoining Conrail trackage at Essay Tower just above South Amboy. Once "OI-60" delivered inbound cars for our customers, the crew switched ends on their locomotives and coupled up to our outbound traffic for Oak Island. The outbound train was then coupled, inspected, and tested so that it was ready when OI-60 arrived.

Teamwork of a different type involved working with our sales department to explore revised service patterns for a customer due to limited onsite capacity at their facility, along with operations constraints due to a major MofW project. After meeting with the Conrail account manager handling the account and our customer, we worked with the terminal superintendent and developed a revised operating plan. I discussed the plan with crew and front-line managers before the plan was implemented — and our customer was pleased that we listened to their concerns and took action.

There were times when service was missed, but by working together, we figured out how to get things done. There are a lot of personalities on the railroad resulting in some internal friction. But we all knew that the customer came first. On Conrail, we worked hard to respect one another and collectively figured out how to get our mission of customer service handled successfully.

Doug Watts works the east end of Frankfort Yard on Tony Koester's HO Nickel Plate layout, bringing his decades of railroad experience along with him. Railroaders are valuable members of modeled operations communities.

CHAPTER FIVE

YARD DESIGN: YOUR LAYOUT AND ITS MISSION

Each of us enjoys different aspects of the hobby, and in a variety of ways. Some prefer building; others enjoy operations or a combination of activities. Regardless of your preferences, before you do a deep dive into planning or building a yard, you need to think like the prototype, **1**. Ask yourself: What is the goal of your railroad, **2**, and how does a yard support that goal?

1 Some yards exist primarily to serve one large industry as was the case in Canton, N.C., where the Blue Ridge Southern Railroad worked to serve the massive paper plant there. Four SD45 rebuilds work together to assemble the outbound road freight on March 30, 2023.

It's time now to take what we've seen and learned in the first four chapters and apply it to our plans for our model railroads: How do we make all this work in a limited space? How can we ensure that what we design meets our goals?

The late Allen McClelland's famous "beyond the basement" concept plays large here. Chances are you're reading this because you are beyond the point of just building whatever fits the space. You're seeing this yard idea as one worth thinking about in the context of your whole railroad. So how does a yard help make your layout achieve your goals, and what's the best way to design what you need?

DEVELOPING A VISION FOR YOUR RAILROAD

Why do you model what you model? Are you fascinated with a certain era of railroad history, with steam engines or perhaps the variety and complexity of railroading in the transition era, **3**? Are you interested in one particular railroad and its operations or equipment? Perhaps it's the awe and wonder you felt in your youth seeing trains with eyes wide open, full of excitement and curiosity and utter fascination, **4**. Or, perhaps the modern scene has caught your eye, with the technological innovations and immediacy of the sights of today's railroads with huge trains and remote-control locomotives, pushing machines to their limits, **5**.

Your layout offers any of these opportunities for you to set a vision and then to build that vision into a working railroad. It is that overall vision that will help you decide how yards fit into your scheme.

CAR CLASSIFICATION

Most model railroads that have any plan for operating trains should have at least one yard for classifying cars. Starting with this idea, we can look at a few prototype examples and distill their most critical functions to our layouts. Any yard used for classification will have some key design elements that help to guide the planning and design efforts.

Such a yard need not be massive. It depends on the trains you plan to run:

Coal has been a dominant source of traffic since the early 1800s, and the Norfolk & Western was one of the best at moving it. The huge yard at Bluefield, W.V., was designed to classify coal loads by destination and hold the trains for movement east. The sign says it all. Today, the traffic base is more mixed, as evidenced by the manifest freight shown above.

What's your typical train length? Are trains leaving blocks for other trains, **6**? Is there an interchange?

Yards used for prototype classification range from small to vast, from a handful of tracks to hundreds. All but the largest model railroads are significantly limited by space and therefore small- and medium-sized yards are the ones most commonly modeled. From small to huge, though, each yard employs a series of turnouts ("yard ladder") to access multiple parallel tracks to which cars with the same (or similar) destinations are sorted, **7**.

Part of car classification is blocking. Blocking plays a role not just in ordinary ("loose-car") freight yards but also an extensive role in intermodal modeling. If you model prototype railroading since the 1920s, as Chapter 3 explained, blocking is going to be part of the operational scheme behind how you run trains, **8, 9**. Simply put, blocks are how all the major railroads group cars for movement. On a model railroad, we need running tracks (arrival and departure tracks) to ensure smooth operations into and out of the yard. We need to ensure that tracks are accessible from both directions to hold an entire block of cars inbound or outbound, **10, 11**. Many well-known model railroads captured this well. A good example, and one who operates regularly, is Sammy Carlisle, who models the Santa Fe in 1994 and 1995. His operation at Clovis, N.M., is a slice of how the prototype moved blocks of cars — see "Block exchange on the Transcon" featuring his layout on page 62).

FREIGHT TERMINALS

The large stub-ended yards we discussed in Chapter 2 are unique facilities that deserve mention here. For everyone that enjoys the rail/marine interface with cargo cranes, ferry, or tug-and-barge car float or wharf operations, this is for you! Large classification bowls are usually present where entire inbound trains are brought in and then classified as needed for the outbound move. Bulk loads may be sorted for unloading or for loading onto ferries, while loose-car shipments are sorted to different tracks and grouped by destination much in the same way they would be for outbound trains. But in the case of rail/marine operations, cars are loaded onto ferries or barges for movement across a body of water to railheads on the other side. For modern modelers, too, car floats still exist, **12**. Terminals offer all sorts of exciting opportunities for modeling.

INDUSTRIAL SWITCHING

Almost every model railroad has online industries with customers modeled in

3 With brand-new Alcos on the ready tracks at a formerly all-steam facility, the transition era is well underway, despite the steam yard switcher in the distance at Frankfort Yard on Tony Koester's HO Nickel Plate.

4 Early inspirations for my Conrail Onondaga Cutoff layout came from regular childhood visits to DeWitt Yard in Central New York. Here I, Matt Dean, Jack Trabachino, and Ben Abeles visit the shops in July 1990: childhood memories drive a powerful sense of place in model railroading. *Susie Dean Abeles*

5 CSX is a huge coal-hauling Class I railroad. Eastbound export loads depart Cumberland Yard at Mexico Tower at Baltimore, Md., on Aug. 8, 2014.

6 Montana Rail Link's small yard facility at Logan, Mont., hosts a local freight, the 844, that takes blocks dropped off by other trains and spots cars on several branch lines as well as around town as needed. Small yards are used for classification, too.

one fashion or another. Yards designed specially for industrial switching include several additional features in addition to those discussed above. A great variety of online industries can even support a yard of their own — steel mills, coal mines, power plants, large grain complexes, chemical plants, paper mills, and automobile factories and unloading areas each are large enough to easily justify an entire yard, **13, 14, 15, 16**. Other examples are described in detail in Tony Koester's book *Space-Saving Industries For Your Layout* (Kalmbach).

PASSENGER OPERATIONS

Often overlooked are passenger yards, often called coach yards, which were common into the 1960s before Amtrak. Very much their own entity, passenger operations require different resources and a different design approach on the prototype because the pattern of operation is different than that of most freight trains. Large and regional passenger yards must provide not only storage of equipment but also the ability to service cars — and sometimes entire train sets — between runs. Classification of individual cars is not as common as with regular freight, but the addition of Pullman sleepers, baggage/mail cars, and express and express refrigerator service to your operations can add multiple "industries" to be switched and served. And don't forget cleaning, inspection, maintenance, and supply facilities to ready cars for the next run.

If you are still in the layout-planning stage, don't forget that a number of U.S. cities were key interchange points for passenger service. Especially

7 This view looks down the ladder track at Glenwood Yard on the Allegheny Valley Railroad, part of the Carload Express System that operates several short lines in the Pittsburgh area. The green targets at left on the hand-throw turnouts tell crews that those switches are lined for the normal (straight) route and the yellow shows a switch that's lined for the reverse (diverging) route. *Rich Wisneski*

8 The yard at Black Hawk on Doug Tagsold's Colorado & Southern has just three yard tracks where blocks can be arranged and stored for pick up. Immediately behind the yard is an industrial spur with four customers. Number 70 assembles its train for the return trip to Denver; in the distance is the small engine facility, which includes a turntable, three-stall roundhouse, and coaling tower. *Doug Tagsold*

The C&S Yard at Golden, Colo., on Doug Tagsold's layout is quite small, with the main line and a passing siding in front of the depot, plus two yard tracks. Although the yard is small, there are numerous industrial spurs radiating out to the various Golden customers, including the Adolph Coors brewery in the distance. Today engine No. 74 works the local customers and builds its train for its daily run to Denver. Doug Tagsold

Butler Yard on the New York, Susquehanna & Western is a busy blocking yard serving trains entering and leaving the northern New Jersey area. Jerry Dziedzic's operation also uses the yard per the prototype to meet the single-car passenger train with freights as needed. Flat areas to the left at the edge of the layout allow for operators to place paperwork in a location that keeps track clear and scenery in one piece.

through the transition era, many long-distance trains included cars (especially sleepers and express cars) destined for multiple destinations, often on a connecting railroad. Many cities hosted complex passenger switching operations, requiring trains to set out and pick up coaches, Pullmans, express cars, and diners, **17**. Even a simple depot can serve as a small (passenger service) switching yard, **18**.

Service planning for passenger operations is an art unto itself, with the goal of turning cars around quickly to minimize the amount of equipment needed, **19**. A significant part of that planning is figuring out how to efficiently clean, fuel and inspect locomotives and how to get the passenger cars ready for their next assignment.

MAINTENANCE AND STORAGE

While the basic purpose of yards is to keep cars moving, they also have dedicated tracks to store cars or trains for future movement or planned work. This can be an older, smaller yard converted to car (or even locomotive) storage or a dedicated track or two in a larger yard holding cars awaiting assignment from local agencies. On our model railroads we can sometimes add a track or two here and there to hold equipment not in current use — and who among us doesn't have some great-looking equipment that we're not immediately using?

There are a variety of creative, yet plausible, ways to do this. One example is simply modeling a storage yard. Storage of rarely-used equipment is common on the prototype. Maintenance equipment such as snowplows, Jordan spreaders, flangers, tool cars, bunk cars, and scale test cars is very common in yard areas. Even better, much maintenance-of-way (MoW) equipment is often older equipment no longer used in revenue service, such as gondolas, boxcars converted into

Sparta Junction on Jerry Dziedzic's railroad is a critical and busy location where the NYS&W main line crosses the Lehigh & Hudson River main at a universal interlocking, with a small interchange yard adjacent to both. Central of New Jersey power (left) running through on the L&HR works around a local that's dropping a block of cars for pickup later by the NYS&W.

tool cars, and old coaches converted into crew cars. In the period following many mergers, these storage areas could host a variety of cars from predecessor roads as well as different variations of paint schemes. Out-of-service revenue equipment can also be stored at the edge of yard areas and can be conveniently tucked into some of the tighter spaces.

WHERE DO WE GO FROM HERE?

All of these features and types of yards apply to model railroads. Think of how your trains will run and what sort of interactions they will have. The yards you choose will be crossroads and gathering places for your trains, helping connect your railroad to the world beyond your layout.

Missouri Pacific maintained a carfloat operation on the Mississippi River at Natchez, Miss., as late as the early 1980s. Under hot summer sun, MoPac GP18 1883 moves cars down to the float barge (left). Above, once on the barge lead, the locomotive is kept off the barge itself by using spacer (idler) cars. Two photos: Jerry Dziedzic

Alleghany Ludlum Steel Co. maintains an extensive industrial switching railroad that runs right along public roads in Natrona, Pa. One of the company's "critters" pushes empty slag cars back into the plant on July 23, 2013, with the yard serving the facility beyond.

Eastman Chemical's massive network of plants around Kingsport, Tenn., employs a number of leased switching locomotives along with dedicated jobs from both CSX and Norfolk Southern. This huge pinwheel yard sorts tank cars 24 hours a day, 7 days a week.

15 Belvidere & Delaware River serves local customers via a Norfolk Southern interchange at Hudson Yard in Phillipsburg, N.J., on Oct. 19, 2017.

16 Details in our modeled yards are extra noticeable in yards where crews will spend time. Here crews work to attach outbound blocks of cars to yard air lines at East Yard on Bill Darnaby's proto-freelanced HO Maumee Route. Bill Darnaby

17

Passenger cars get switched and interchanged, too. Union Pacific sleeper *Arden* is part of an Erie Lackawanna through train to the west at Hoboken, N.J. on October 17, 1964. Rich Taylor

Small-town depots are also places where passenger trains on certain routes set out or pick up cars. On the Maumee Route, Lafontaine Depot has a house track for business cars and setouts of Pullmans, express cars, and baggage cars. These operations were quite common through the 1950s. Bill Darnaby

18

19

Locomotives are turned at St. Louis Union Station — one of the country's busiest passenger terminals into the 1960s — for an outbound run back home to the Wabash. Complicated trackwork is a matter of course for most major passenger terminals, including complex installations like the double-slip switches to the right of the locomotive. Rich Taylor

BLOCK EXCHANGE ON THE TRANSCON: CLOVIS YARD ON THE SANTA FE HEREFORD SUBDIVISION // By Sammy Carlile

Santa Fe GP60M No. 125 leads today's hot 198 train into Clovis for a crew change. The 198 was a daily Chicago-Los Angeles hotshot on the Transcon, and its priority was expedited trailer traffic for carriers such as United Parcel Service, the U.S. Postal Service, and J.B. Hunt. Other trains in this scene include (from foreground), V-LAMC (empty auto racks to McCook, Ill.); 893 (hotshot intermodal to Kansas City); H-FRSR (wine and canned goods from Fresno, Calif., to a Conrail connection at Streator, Ill.); and S-LBCK (K-Line containers from Long Beach, Calif., to Kansas City). All are based on prototype Santa Fe trains operating during the summer of 1995. All are ready for crews to take them eastward to Amarillo, Texas.
Sammy Carlile

My model railroad represents the Atchison, Topeka & Santa Fe's Hereford subdivision in the summer of 1995. After I had hosted several operating sessions and had finally worked up a balanced operations plan for the trains on my layout, I turned my attention to my version of Clovis (N.M.) Yard, at the western end of my layout. Most of this yard serves as a visible staging yard for eastbound trains, and I've done my best to add scenery and some additional operational interest to it.

The prototype is a block-swapping yard, which operates a bit differently than a common freight classification yard. Going eastward, Clovis was the last stop on the narrow part of the ATSF "funnel" before the main line split in two directions. East of Clovis, the bulk of the trains take the famed Transcon line which heads northeast toward Amarillo, Kansas City, and Chicago, with their connections to Eastern trunk lines. The other line heads southeast to Texas — to Lubbock, Dallas/Fort Worth, and Houston, along with connections that lead to southeastern states. Thus, Clovis is where many eastbound trains stopped to swap blocks of intermodal freight into other trains bound for different destinations. I spent some time in the mid-1990s on my travels through Clovis and I'd always listen to the yard crews on the scanner. Switch engines in the yard operated around the clock, moving cars and blocks from train to train.

I later came across a copy of one of the last ATSF system operating plans which provided more-detailed information such as train schedules and the blocks each train usually carried. This also explained what the various trains typically did at each terminal. On my layout, westbound road crews stop at the western end of the Clovis depot platform for a simulated crew change. A member of the yard crew then takes the train and runs it around the Melrose return loop, transforming it into an eastbound train when it reaches West Clovis. The train then enters the western end of the yard.

The yardmaster has a copy of the train lineup and a copy of the train list that shows which trains drop off blocks. All types of trains call at Clovis. For example, the eastbound S-LACH (Stacks — double-stack container cars — Los Angeles to Chicago) has a block of cars that drop at Clovis for movement to St Louis on Q-CVLI (Quality Intermodal, Clovis to Lindenwood Yard in St. Louis). The switch crew will pick these cars off S-LACH and put them in a storage track. Eastbound Q-LANY (Los Angeles to New York) also has a block of cars that goes to St Louis, so the exercise is repeated a short time later in the session. The Q-CVLI originates in Clovis and is entirely made up of these two blocks. The Clovis yardmaster assigns power, builds the train, and runs it into an empty yard track. It's then added to the dispatcher's sheet to be crewed and run eastward toward Amarillo later in the session. This sequence is repeated with a few other intermodal trains that also drop small blocks of cars.

The Clovis yard crew makes a switching move near the west end of the yard. They've pulled these three company-service diesel fuel tanks from the H-HOBA (Houston-Barstow) train. This train originated at Houston and since the railroad gets a better rate on fuel there, it ships it on manifest trains to distant points such as Clovis and Belen, N.M.
Sammy Carlile

Another train of interest is an intermodal train that terminates in Clovis and splits into two separate blocks. One block becomes its own complete train that turns into the Q-CVTL (Clovis to Tulsa). The other block is a group of empty auto racks that are added to the V-LAMC (Los Angeles to McCook, Ill.) train for forwarding to the Chicago area, where they are interchanged to Canadian National (former Grand Trunk Western) for the trip to Detroit.

For non-intermodal traffic, there is also a manifest train that comes to Clovis from Houston (the H-HOBA) carrying loads of diesel fuel for the locomotive terminal. This is a quick reduce-and-fill before the train returns back to the Lubbock staging yard as the H-BAHO. To help round out the manifest traffic, another manifest train terminates in Clovis with the first half of the train becoming the local road switcher that heads toward Hereford and returns. The other half of the inbound train is a block of grain covered hoppers that are combined with 14 more hoppers from a nearby grain elevator to become a grain train bound for Houston and Galveston.

All of these functions come together in a time frame of about 3½ actual hours in a typical operating session. My version of Clovis Yard mimics what the prototype did on a daily basis and it makes for busy and action-packed yard operation — another day on the Santa Fe.

Clovis yardmaster Dave Salamon ponders his next moves working the West end of Clovis Yard on the lower deck of Sammy's Santa Fe Hereford Sub. He's already pulled two loaded well cars of J.B. Hunt containers (lower right) from the S-LACH train to be forwarded to St. Louis on the Q-CVLI. Sammy Carlile

Clovis yardmaster Jay Hastings has two cars for St. Louis routed back through the crossover as he shoves them into a storage track. Two more intermodal trains will be along within the next few hours, each with a block of cars for St Louis. Once all three of the blocks have been assembled, Clovis will add the road power to the train, move the train into a staging track, and then notify the dispatcher that the train is ready to be added to the lineup to run eastward. Sammy Carlile

Samuel Carlile is on the head end of the S-LACH train and Jay Hastings is on the Clovis switch engine. The switcher makes a quick move and grabs the two loaded well cars and pulls them into the clear. Samuel will then back the train up, recouple, then pull the train into a staging track for movement eastward toward Chicago later in the session. The two cars picked from the train will be moved into a storage track until additional cars going to St. Louis arrive and are added to the cut. Sammy Carlile

CHAPTER SIX

YARD DESIGN AND CONSTRUCTION

Layout space: Does anyone have exactly the space — size and shape — they'd like for their model railroad? In almost every dimension, we have less room than we'd like for our layouts. Everything in modeling seems to be a compromise, an adaptation of what prototype railroads do. It seems a burden to always be considering ways to downsize the footprint of the prototype, but even the smallest yards on the prototype represent more real estate than many of us have for an entire layout, **1**.

1 Conrail train COSE has finished its work as dawn breaks at my HO Conrail Onondaga Yard, and the train now heads east onto the main line at CP 280 on Oct. 4, 1994. Mainline operations helped determine what had to be included at Onondaga on my layout and also showed what could be compromised.

However, we have the choice to replicate key elements of yards that we can research and selectively incorporate into our track and layout plans. The physical limits of our available areas can help focus our efforts on what matters most, helping us decide which key design elements of a yard we should include and what we can let go.

In the early 2000s, Model Railroader editor and highly regarded model yardmaster Andy Sperandeo (Andy *loved* running yards during operating sessions) authored a book on model railroad yards that opened many eyes to yard concepts. It provided great ideas on how to create a yard that would serve its intended purpose. Several of his key ideas are worth repeating:

1. Yards work best when cars keep moving. Remember, freight cars don't belong sitting in a yard — they should be moving freight and earning revenue. Yards are great places to classify cars so they can more efficiently move in outbound trains to their destinations, **2**.

2. Pay attention to yard elements. The interplay between elements — track spacing, ladder-track design, turnout frog numbers, and yard-track length — is fascinating and related. When space is tight, consider a ladder arrangement other than a straight ladder — compound ladders, pinwheel ladders and ladders on the angle of the next smaller frog number all can help maximize yard capacity (see page 75).

3. A switching lead ("drill track") should be included and should be longer than the longest body track in the yard. This enables a switch or drill crew to pull an entire track for classification without tying up other tracks, helping to expedite classification — and therefore yard operations, **3**.

4. Give a name to every track, both at entrances to the yard and throughout the yard itself. In fact, name every track on the rest of your layout, too. Protype railroads name each track; a common language of named tracks aids in operations and generates a sense or feel of a working railroad, **4**.

5. Avoid interference: Design the yard to accommodate inbound and outbound trains without interfering with yard switchers. Track layouts that are most effective allow parallel moves or include drill leads off the main line so through traffic has a place to wait while a pickup or setout is made, **5**. The fewer interruptions for the yard crews, the better!

6. A staging yard is a way to represent "beyond the basement" — the world beyond our railroads, a "somewhere else" to which our operations are directly linked. Staging provides a home for traffic that is headed offline or would be coming from offline, whether it be another railroad or another subdivision of the railroad we model.

7. Paperwork is part of every prototype operation. Switch lists should use the name of the tracks in the yard. Whether you choose lists or car cards, you will save time and confusion if you can handle cars in sequence as they arrive and are classified to outbound blocks. Allow space for a shelf, pull-out desk, or small table for paperwork for your train crews, **6, 7, 8**.

2 The Duluth, Missabe & Iron Range moved all sorts of trains but it was built to move iron ore and, later, taconite pellets. Big 2-8-8-4 No. 227 is on the pull from High Grade Yard in Bovey, Minn., on Bob Hanmer's railroad under the watchful eye of engineer Rich Remiarz. The ore will head to docks on Lake Superior and then by boat to the furnaces of steel mills in the Midwest.

3 Prototype railroads include long yard leads to allow tracks to be pulled while staying off the main line, allowing through trains to pass without interference from yard switching. Chicago & North Western No. 4253, part of an experimental rebuild program using Cummins diesel engines on EMD chassis, pulls a cut of cars. The rebuilds didn't work out, but the switching leads are still around! *Al Tillotson*

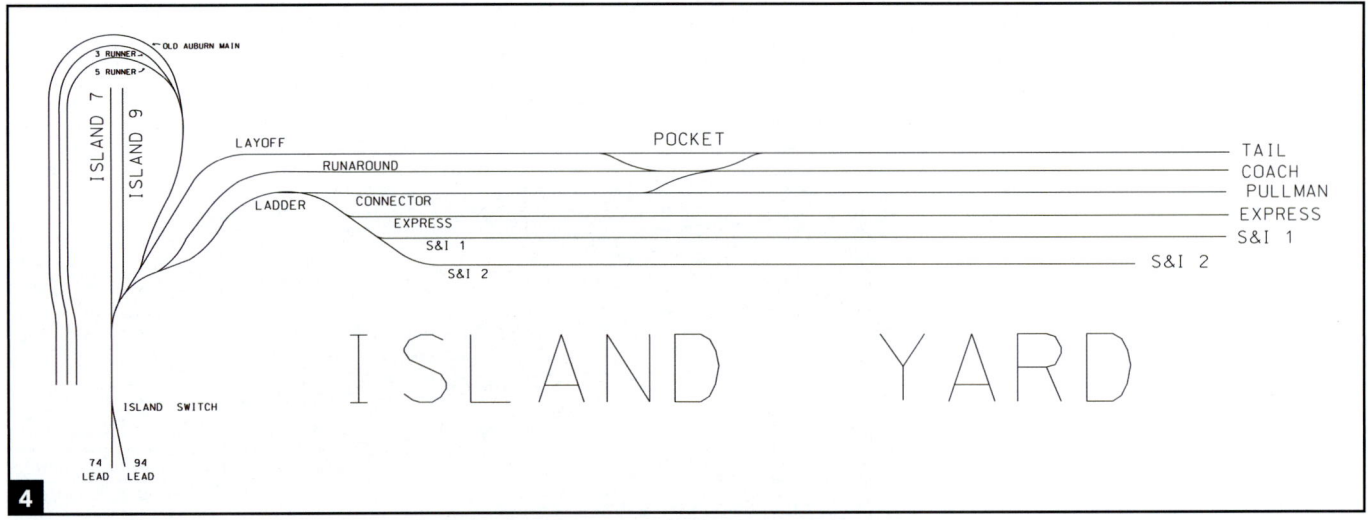

4 Here's a schematic drawing of Island Yard on my Onondaga Cutoff, showing track names. Naming tracks on your railroad is important — on the prototype, every track (and even every potential switching spot on the track) has a name, enabling clear communication between crews.

5 Proctor Yard on Canadian National's former Duluth, Missabe & Iron Range includes long yard leads to allow switchers to work without interfering with passing freights. Here limestone loads head for the taconite plants of Minnesota's iron range in September 2006. The gray area between rails is spilled taconite pellets.

8. Sort cars by where they go next. Don't worry about the old adage of "touch a car once." Unless you have an extremely large yard, the next outbound cut is more important than how many times you handle a car.

9. Interchange increases interest in yard operations. Locate your yard close to a junction with a branch line or short line to facilitate interchange moves and analyze inbound cars with their connections to outbound trains. If you have no room for a visible connection, you can model an interchange with a train running from and returning to staging — from a yard operations perspective, the important thing is the handoff between two railroads, **9**.

10. Assign several operators to major yards. In addition to a yardmaster to direct operations, you'll have a switch crew or two and perhaps a hostler or additional crews to run engine facilities and keep trains moving.

11. Follow your prototype, but focus on double-ended yards. Yes, they take more room, but yards with ladders at each end are not only more common on the prototype, they allow greater flexibility in operations and in handing trains in both directions. Double-ended yards can be worked from both ends simultaneously. Just as on the prototype, double-ended yards move cars faster, which can help the traditional imbalance between shorter (and therefore disproportionately faster) mainline runs and the relatively slow speed of flat switching. The hard reality is that model trains cover typical compressed layout distances a lot faster than a crew can flat-switch cars, so anything you can do to speed yard operations helps avoid clogged yards and idle road crews (not to mention congestion in the aisles).

PHYSICAL CHARACTERISTICS

First things first: yards are created to serve a certain purpose. What purpose will your yard be filling for your railroad? As we saw in Chapter 5, much of what you are looking for in a modeled yard will be guided by how that yard fits your railroad. While prototype designs are often restricted based on available real estate, modelers tend to have even harder limits with available space. It can seem frustrating when you begin laying things out. Yard ladders and turnouts always seem to need a longer area than originally envisioned. How can we compromise to get what we need in the space we have?

The best way to begin — as is the case with the rest of the railroad — is with a drawing or track plan. Drawing allows us to visualize the ideas we have in our minds, and allows us to adjust and think through the various track elements and how all will fit, **4**, **10**.

Start with a scale drawing of the layout space. This can be done by hand, using a scale rule where a certain measurement is equal to a foot, or it can be done digitally on a computer

Bob Rodriguez's Nickel City Yard includes a full desk area and remote video cameras for operations on his Nickel City Lines. It's important to give crews and yardmasters a space for paperwork, so they can stay organized without being tempted to use the layout itself as a desk.

At a minimum, be sure to include clips and hangers for paperwork. If you use car cards, mount boxes in a convenient spot at yards and towns. This is Hornell Yard on Perry Squier's Pittsburg, Shawmut & Northern.

Perry's St. Marys yardmaster location includes a large panel with toggle switches to throw turnouts. The bottom ledge provides a good place to temporarily park paperwork. Note also the block-line telephone and a mount for throttles.

9 Modeling interchanges adds visual and operational interest. Many cars and are handed to another railroad for part of their trip. The Minoa & Euclid (a subsidiary of the Morristown & Erie) interchanges with Conrail at Onondaga Yard on my layout.

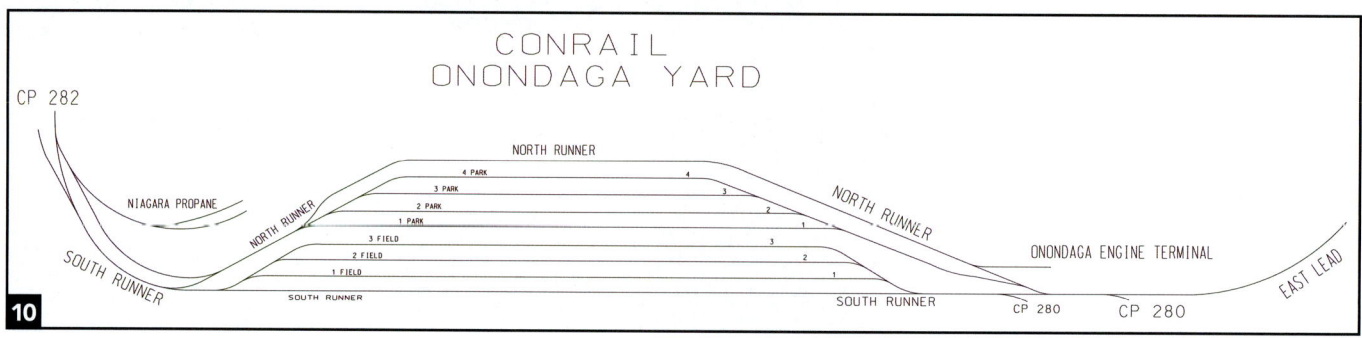

10 During the early planning process for my layout, I prepared a working sketch of Onondaga Yard on CAD software. It allowed for easy discussion among fellow modelers interested in the design. The main line was not included on this early drawing.

with track planning software. Atlas offers track planning software, as do several other sources. You can also use AutoCAD, Microstation, or other software packages with which you're familiar. Once the layout space is defined, you can see what you have to work with and begin to make decisions.

One possibility is to print out the plans in full scale and lay them on the floor, **11**. Tom Schmieder did this as he was in the early planning stages for Port Morris Yard on his Delaware, Lackawanna & Western. He began with the prototype track diagram, redrew it to fit, then printed it to scale and tested the prints on the floor of the layout room. With some tweaks, it fit, offering construction a firm plan to begin. If you can't make a full-size printout, use photocopies of actual track components.

It's worth this extra time and effort in the planning stage, because the effort and expense to create a yard is a big one. Moving track that was already laid is a time-consuming task; moving turnouts in particular can result in damaged components. It's better to make mistakes and make changes when things are in drawing form rather than wait and have to deal with mistakes later.

Any drawing will need some basic assumptions to start. Thankfully, many have walked this path before (and made mistakes and learned from them), leaving a series of "constants" for the rest of us to use as guidelines. Here are a few key guidelines:

TRACK SPACING

Prototype yards have parallel tracks (with concentric curves, as needed) to maximize use of space. The distance between those tracks is determined by the geometry of the turnouts used and by the needs of the yard. Classification yards, for example, might have center-to-center spacing of 12 feet. Intermodal yards might be wider — 40 feet on center — or even have pairs of closely spaced tracks with a wide pathway in between to allow access for rubber-tired cranes and trucks between tracks to load and unload trailers and containers.

Modern arrival and departure yards are often constructed with enough distance between tracks for a paved access lane, **12**. On the prototype, most yards make use of tighter switch geometry than main lines, possible because speeds are lower in yards. The same applies with curves. The tight S-curves created by adjacent turnouts must be

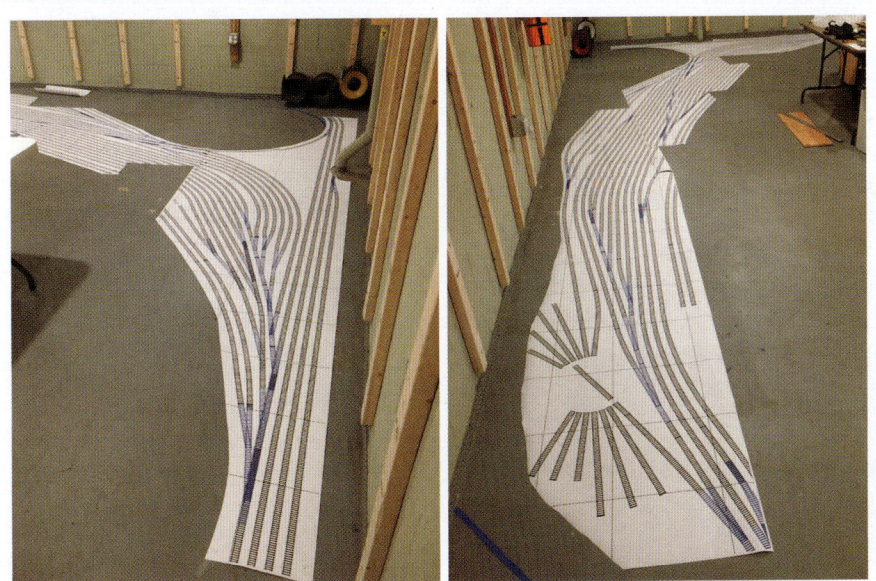

11 Tom Schmieder drew his planned Port Morris, N.J., yard in HO to scale, then printed it out full size to see how it fit the space. At left is the east end; at right, the west end includes a turntable — more easily planned at full size!

considered, but the higher the switch frog number, the less those S-curves impact operations. Our modeling follows suit. Use of No. 5 or No. 6 switches is common in modeled yards. See veteran modeler Andy Sperandeo's thoughts on ladders and spacing on page 75.

Our yards need to be as long as feasible, so in many cases we'll use curved turnouts or space-saving switches as needed to maximize length and number of tracks, **13**, **14**. While stub-ended yards allow for more storage, they are operationally more limited than double-ended yards — each can be useful depending on the specific situation and the traffic flow.

TRACK NAMING AND LABELING

As mentioned earlier, nearly every track on a prototype railroad has a unique name or designation. Whether a number or an actual name, the identifier ensures that crew members know the specific tracks being referred to in conversations with each other, with dispatchers, or other workers such as maintenance or management personnel. If you've ever listened in on railroaders' radio conversations, you know that a crew member spotting cars doesn't say "put the cars over there" or point to a spot on a track and say "move those cars here." Instead, they say "spot the car on the runaround" or "move those cars over to the North Runner." Specific names and spots ensure everyone is on the same page. Not only is that much more efficient, but it's safer as well.

Once your modeled tracks are named, turn your attention to how those names are communicated to your crews and visitors, **15**. Railroaders take time to memorize the characteristics of the railroads over which they operate, and the company makes available maps and diagrams to help with that process. You can use simple diagrams, labels, and signs mounted on the edge of the layout (on the fascia) to show a track diagram for an area and include the names for each track present, **16**. However you decide to handle it, it's important to make these convenient and visible so that crews can become familiar with the name of each yard track and use them regularly.

TURNOUT CONTROL

How you decide to control the turn-

12 Distant headlights announce the arrival of eastbound trains into the eastbound run-through yard at Union Pacific's massive Bailey Yard in North Platte, Neb., as coal and stack trains prepare to depart. Modern yards are typically built with wider track spacing than those in the steam and transition eras, allowing rubber-tired utility vehicles to have easy and safe access.

13 Customized trackwork is still used in 2023 in passenger and even freight yards when the need warrants. Modern oil and coal trains still use this three-way turnout in Utah Railway's Martin (Utah) Yard.

14 RJ Corman operates shortline railroads across the eastern U.S., including this historic route from Middlesboro, Ky., through the Cumberland Gap tunnel to Tennessee. The yard is hemmed in by the town, and the layout of turnouts reflects the tight nature of the available land.

outs in your yard affects your crews in how they operate trains in the yard. Once again, we look to the prototype, where control can either be electrical from the cab or dispatcher office, electric or pneumatic from a tower, or manually by the crew on the ground at the turnout.

On my Onondaga Cutoff, I elected to use manual ground throws for all yard tracks, while interlocked switches are controlled by electric machines, **17**. I made exceptions on some turnouts that would be hand-thrown on the prototype but on the layout are not easily reachable from the aisles. For those difficult-to-reach spots, I used Tortoise switch machines controlled by simple toggle switches mounted to the fascia. The toggles are labeled to match the names of the tracks to ensure clarity for crews.

Other modelers have come up with some ingenious ways to control turnouts. Some use toggles and switch machines for all turnouts, even those along the front edge of the yard. Some use mechanical levers below the layout, with a fascia-mounted handle connected to the turnout using stiff wire. (Several versions of these manual throws are available commercially.) The important thing is that the points are held firmly in place so that equipment moves across them without derailment.

YARD LIMITS

Most modelers are familiar with the "yard limit" signs seen in photos and along the right of way of many railroads. Rule 93 in the *General Code of Operating Rules* (GCOR) establishes yard limits as a term for a rule affecting the main track next to a yard and requires that all trains (except first class

Above: To casual observers, the west end of Onondaga Yard presents a pair of ladder tracks, two running tracks, and some crossovers — but to crews, these are the Park Yard and Field Yard, flanked by the North Runner and South Runner running tracks. Below: A yard map with names clearly indicates which track is which.

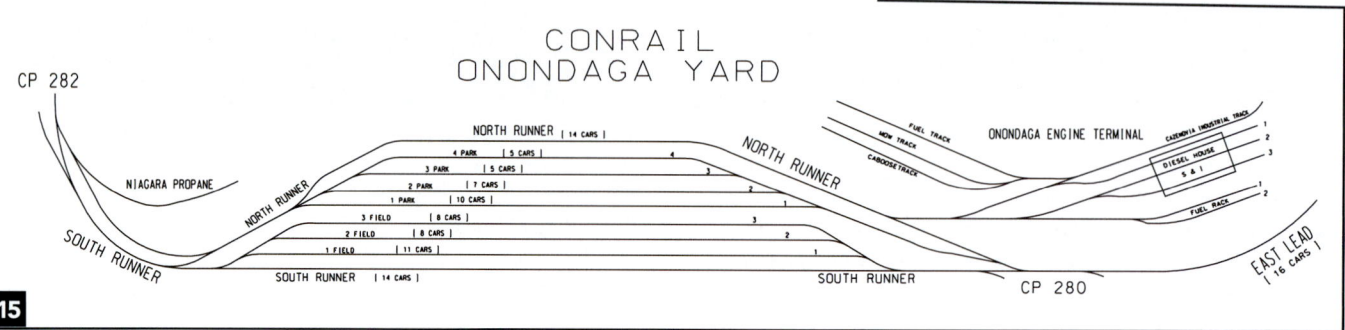

15

trains) in the timetable must approach the yard limit prepared to operate at yard speeds unless the main track is known to be clear. Yard limit signs vary by railroad, but the locations of the signs tell crews the limits in which movements on the main line must operate at yard speeds, looking out for misaligned switches or trains and cars on the tracks ahead, **18**.

The concept of yard limits and Rule 93 was widely used in the era before Centralized Traffic Control (CTC) and automatic block signals. Essentially Rule 93 allows yard and local crews to use the main track without special permission as long as they clear for any first-class timetable scheduled train.

As the use of signals and CTC has become far more common on main tracks, the use of yard limits has declined because under CTC rules the dispatcher or operator must authorize movement into and occupation of a track.

YARD LEADS

Since classification yards are designed to move cars, not store them, it is critical to ensure that a switching locomotive can continue to perform its job moving among the ladder tracks without fouling the main track or route. The "yard lead" or switching lead, a long track extending from the yard ladder, enables this. The yard lead allows a switcher to move freely along the ladder while other trains can still move past on the main track. If the yard ladder connects directly to the main line and other trains need to use the main line, then yard work will be interrupted unless you also provide a dedicated lead for switching.

Yard lead tracks can be configured in a variety of ways. See page 74 for examples of how some well-known model railroad yard leads are laid out. Look at how the yard leads are placed in relation to ladder tracks, how the turnouts are laid out, where yard tracks are connected to the main line, and the location of engine service and rolling stock maintenance areas.

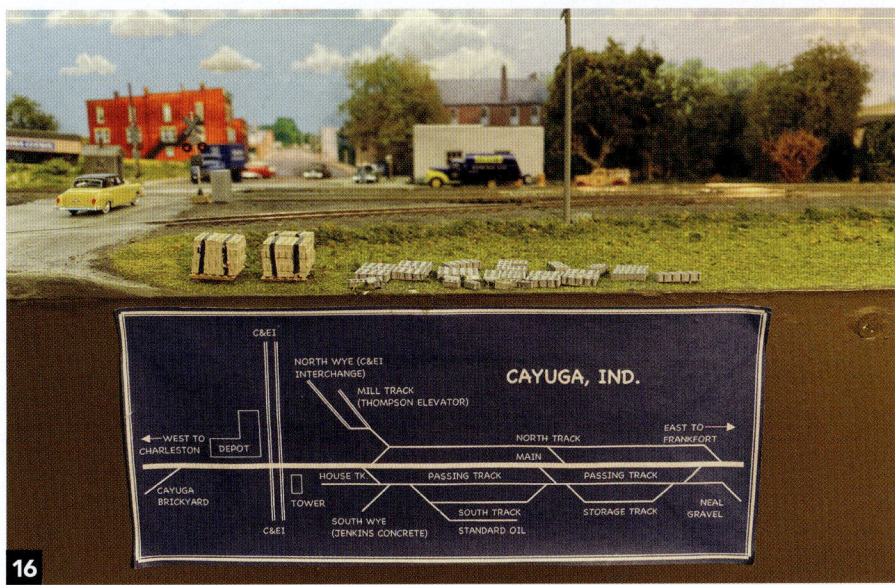

Each town along Tony Koester's HO Nickel Plate layout includes a blueprint diagram on the fascia showing the track and industry diagram. Even the small yard at Cayuga, Ind., has a diagram with track names readily apparent. The maps provide prototype period atmosphere as well as information for crews.

Turnouts in my Onondaga Yard are controlled by ground throws, just as they are in prototype Conrail yards. Road freights and locals alike use the trackage, and crews must watch out ahead for misaligned turnouts.

Rule 93 describes yard limit rules and appropriate signs on most railroads. The approach to East Yard on Bill Darnaby's Maumee Route allows the yard switcher to occupy track within the limits set by the signs without dispatcher permission; the switch crew need only clear for the approach of first-class trains. Bill Darnaby

YARD LEADS/SWITCHING LEADS

Yard or switching leads can be worked into tight spaces in many ways. At right, East Yard at LaFontaine, Ohio, on Bill Darnaby's Maumee Route has the lead wrapped around the inside of a curve. It joins the main line at a tower, but includes a stub-ended extension to increase its length. Below: On my Conrail layout, I extended a stub-ended yard lead inside the curved mainline tracks behind the engine terminal at Onandaga Yard. Bottom: Eric Brooman was able to extend a long, straight stub-ended yard lead on the west end of Benton Yard on his HO Utah Belt.

East Yard, Maumee Route

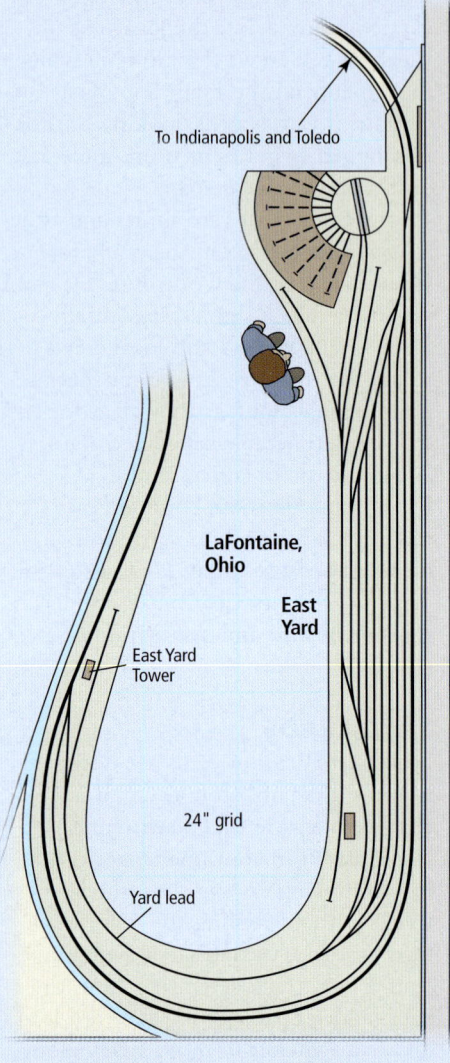

Onandaga Yard, Conrail

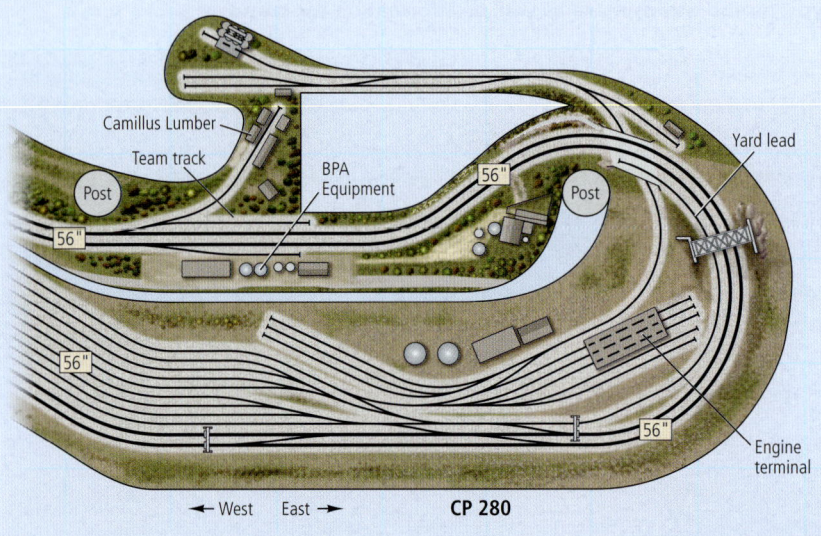

Benton Yard, Utah Belt

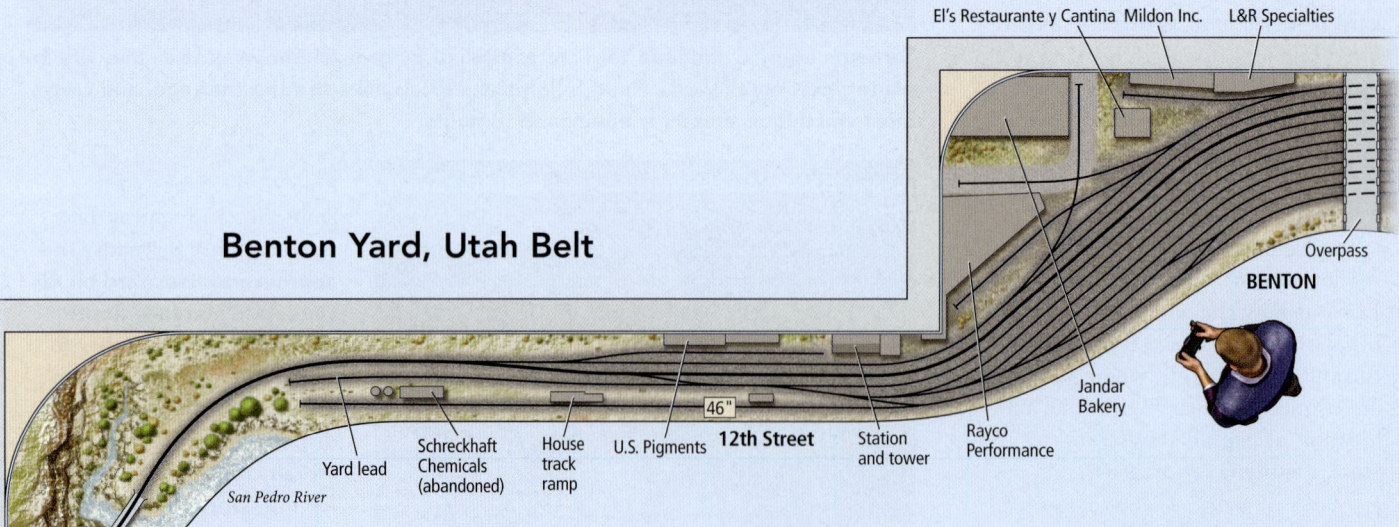

LADDER TRACKS

by Andy Sperandeo

(Excerpted from Andy's book *The Model Railroader's Guide to Freight Yards*)

Railroads prefer straight ladder tracks for safety. There's no need to cross the ladder track to line switches, and engine and ground crews can see each other clearly. For a given frog number, however, these will be the longest ladders and allow the shortest body tracks in the yard.

A common answer to this in the prototype — but one too-rarely used on model railroads—is to set the ladder at a steeper angle than the frogs and continue the curvature of the turnouts past the frogs. A ladder with No. 6 turnouts (frog angle of 9.5 degrees) can be built on the 11.5 degree angle of a No. 5 turnout, with a short but large-radius curve leading into each body track. This gains a few extra car lengths in the body tracks.

More complicated forms can also be used to shorten ladder length. The compound ladder isn't as common in real yards, except for hump yards where the switch points are power operated. With the usual hand-operated turnouts, a compound ladder can require the ground crew to cross active leads, increasing the danger of their work. Where compound ladders are used in flat-switched yards, the switch rods are often extended to allow all the switch stands to be outside the main ladder track, thus reducing the need to cross the ladder while switching.

The pinwheel ladder is even less common on real railroads, but is a useful design tool for modelers. It offers a way to wrap a ladder around the inside of a curve, which in some situations may be the only option for extending body tracks. As long as the turnouts and curve radii are large enough, pinwheel ladders can operate reliably.

With double-ended yards, a common arrangement is to have ladders slope toward each other and toward some theoretical crossing point. This produces "pyramid"-shaped yards, with tracks of decreasing length as you move farther up the ladder. This may not be a problem with only a few tracks or when some classifications will normally see fewer cars than others. The least-used classifications can be assigned to the shortest body tracks and the shortest track of all can be used for the thoroughfare.

For body tracks that are equally long, "diamond-shaped" yards are best. The ladder tracks are parallel, with turnouts branching the same way at both ends of each track. This forms a parallelogram with equal length body tracks.

The St. Marys Yard on Perry Squier's Pittsburg, Shawmut & Northern has a simple ladder that stacks tracks parallel to the main line.

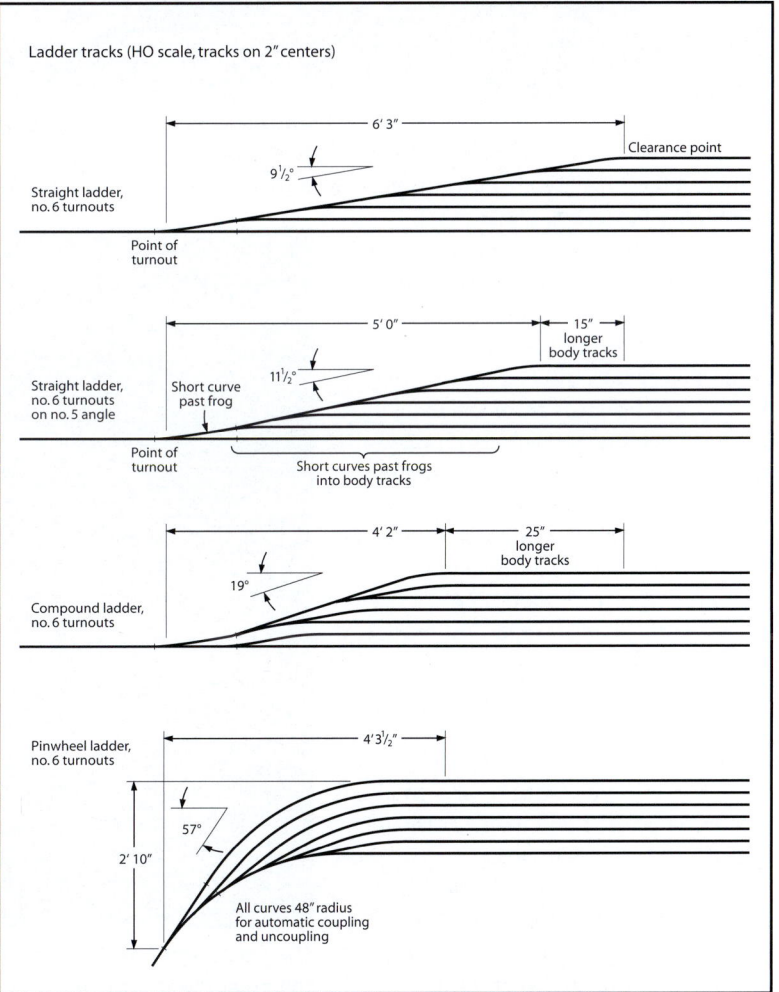

75

CASE STUDY — THE PITTSBURG, SHAWMUT & NORTHERN: MODELING FROM THE PROTOTYPE

Angelica, N.Y., hosted a compact yard on a curve along the Pittsburg, Shawmut & Northern. Perry Squier's yard curves the correct way and includes all major features of the prototype thanks to great research. *Perry Squier collection*

Perry Squier did an amazing amount of research on his favorite prototype, coal-hauler Pittsburg, Shawmut & Northern, which ran in northwestern Pennsylvania and western New York state. His research ultimately resulted in an HO version of the railroad as it existed in 1923.

Perry used photos from the local historical society and railroad historical organizations to start his research. He also made extensive use of maps, including Sanborn Fire Insurance Maps, which were created to document entire towns after about 1866. These are a wealth of information for modelers and are available online for many locales in the Library of Congress (guides.loc.gov/fire-insurance-maps/sanborn). These photos show how Perry adapted key features shown in prototype photos and maps to the design of his model railroad.

You can use Perry's well-executed example as a guide for researching and developing a plan based on your own favorite prototype or yard.

The yard throat at Angelica includes a ladder track that curves off to sidings and the equipment facilities in the yard.

An overview of Angelica captures the remote feeling of the prototype — and the track layout captures the operations.

Perry's Hornell Station and yard are a fantastic facsimile of Hornell, right down to the proper buildings in their places.

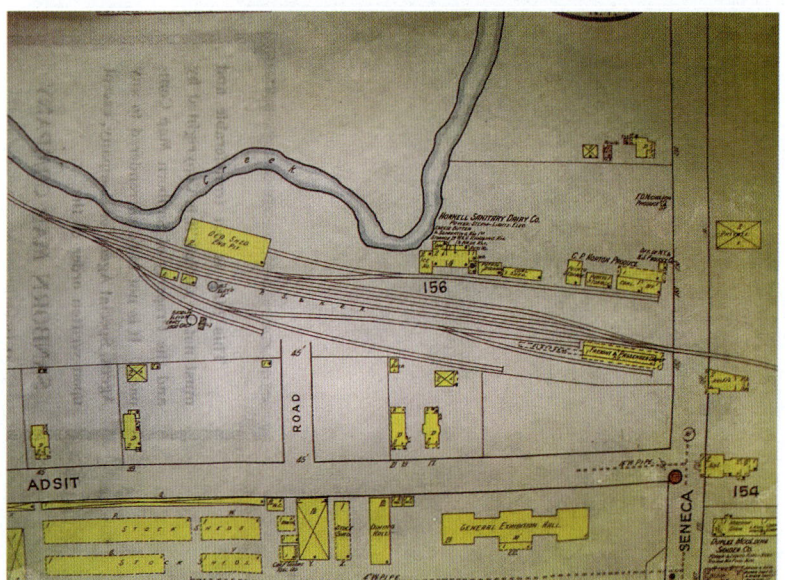

The Sanborn map for Hornell, N.Y., was the starting point for Perry's model of the town's railroad facilities, including the trolley line in the brick-paved street and its diamonds with the PS&N. Sanborn maps include a great deal of detail. Perry Squier collection

Thanks to the size and importance of St. Marys, several good photos exist of the facilities there and Perry was able to use them to scale and scratchbuild many of the structures. Note the yard and freight cars to the left. Perry Squier collection

Perry's model of St. Marys Station captures the look of the prototype very well and is instantly recognizable in the photo above. Such defining structures help a yard develop a sense of place.

An overview of the yard during switching operations shows the layout of the buildings and facilities and gives the impression of a large yard designed to serve the coal and lumber industries that were prevalent in western Pennsylvania and New York.

The well-designed layout of St. Marys yard allows for user conveniences to be included as well. Car-card holders, throttle hangers, uncoupler picks, and the like stand at the ready.

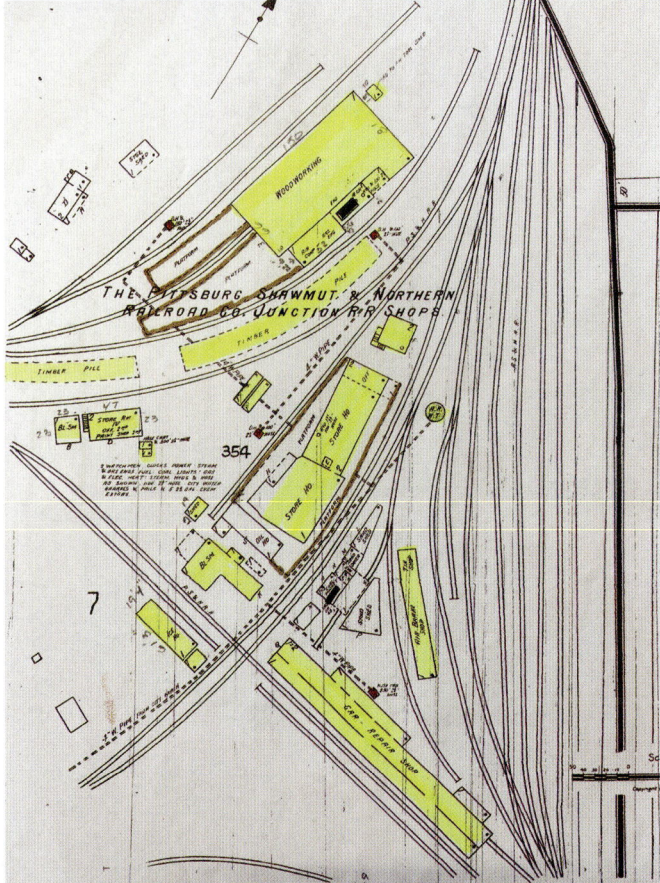

St. Marys Yard is a big junction for the Shawmut, and it follows that it is the centerpiece yard of Perry's railroad. The Sanborn maps again proved their worth by showing the many buildings and their relationship to the railroad — a look Perry captured realistically. *Perry Squier collection*

CHAPTER SEVEN

CAR FORWARDING AND STAGING YARDS

By now you know the basic idea of yards: Cars should not be idle, sitting around for days. Cars are designed to move; prototype railroads earn revenue only when cars are kept moving, **1**. And yet our modeled railroads, although locked in their own space, need to represent the illusion that cars are coming from and going to places beyond the modeled area, **2**.

1

Union Pacific's Bailey Yard in North Platte, Neb., is in a nearly constant state of motion with trains of all types arriving from across the continent, being sorted, and then departing for their destinations. Here coal trains from the Powder River Basin converge at the mainline fuel racks with the expanse of the yard beyond. Matt Van Hattem

We can create this illusion by interweaving active freight yards and staging yards. To me, this is one of the most central themes in model railroading. Your working freight or passenger yards must be designed accordingly and constructed in a way that facilitates moving cars, **3**. Building outbound blocks of cars into trains is a satisfying and fulfilling job. The faster you get the outbounds together, the faster they can head out — leaving your yard with more space to classify the next inbound blocks of cars.

No matter how quickly traffic moves out, the capacity of a yard remains fixed. And the "total capacity" of a yard is always greater than its "functional capacity" — total capacity is the maximum number of cars that will fit, whereas functional capacity is a measure of how many cars can fill the yard without it becoming impossible to work. Keep in mind that yard switching moves become progressively more difficult to make as the yard fills up. On the prototype, cars leaving the yard are of little concern once they're gone. On our layouts, those cars are bound for main lines or staging yards.

ACTIVE YARDS

Thankfully, the prototype is of assistance here as their yard capacities — while far larger than most of ours — are also hard numbers. We can use some of the ideas they employ to monitor car movements on our railroads, too. Prototype railroads over time have developed metrics to measure the effectiveness of yards, and one of the most effective is "average dwell time." This is the average time that a car remains in the yard from arrival to departure. Cars arrive on trains from various points and are then classified into blocks and trains headed to common destinations. Those blocks then wait for pickup by an outbound train. The time from a car's first arrival in the yard through the time the car departs the yard is considered that car's dwell time within the yard, **4**. Add them all up, divide by the number of cars, and you have average dwell time. Prototype dwell times can range from hours to days and present an interesting metric on how "fluid" the traffic flow is on a railroad.

On the prototype, cars are moving from a set origin to a set destination, usually from a factory or warehouse that loads the car (or from the first station where passengers board) to the customer that purchased what was loaded (or to a station where a passenger will de-train). Railroads comprise a

All model railroads deal with space constraints. This overview of the east end of East Yard on Bill Darnaby's Maumee Route shows the yard ladder built on a curve for space reasons. The ladder follows the main line past the yard office and works just as well as a straight ladder, while maximizing space at East Yard. Bill Darnaby

Clovis yardmaster Jay Hastings makes a cut on the S-LACH train at the west end of the yard on Sammy Carlile's Santa Fe Hereford Sub. This train drops a block of J.B. Hunt traffic to move eastward to St Louis on the Q-CVLI train. While both will run through to offline staging, the block exchange is prototypical and adds interest to the function of not just Clovis Yard but the entire railroad. Sammy Carlile

Onondaga Yard - Sorted by Arrival							
Time In	Arriving Train	Car Type	L-E	Cars	Time Out	Departing Train	Dwell
3:30 AM	SEIN	Insulated Box	Empty	2	11:00 AM	ME-1	7:30:00
3:30 AM	SEIN	Plastics	Load	2	5:15 PM	SY1	13:45:00
3:30 AM	SEIN	Diesel Fuel	Load	1	5:15 PM	SY1	13:45:00
3:30 AM	SEIN	Box-Iroquois	Load	2	7:00 PM	ME-2I	15:30:00
3:30 AM	SEIN	Kaolin	Load	2	7:00 PM	ME-2I	15:30:00
3:30 AM	SEIN	Acid/Coal	Load	2	7:00 PM	ME-2I	15:30:00
6:30 AM	COSE	Grain	Load	4	11:00 AM	ME-1	4:30:00
6:30 AM	COSE	CC - Servicing	Empty	1	11:00 AM	ME-1	4:30:00
6:30 AM	COSE	Int	n/a	8	5:15 PM	SY1	10:45:00
10:00 AM	ME-1	Insulated Box	Load	2	8:45 PM	ELSE	10:45:00
10:00 AM	ME-1	CC - Servicing	Empty	1	5:15 PM	SY1	7:15:00
11:45 AM	SY1	Interchange	n/a	3	8:45 PM	ELSE	9:00:00
11:45 AM	SY1	Plastics	Empty	2	12:15 AM	ME2	12:30:00
11:45 AM	SY1	Interchange	n/a	8	1:15 AM	SEEL	13:30:00
11:45 AM	SY1	Interchange	n/a	5	4:15 AM	SEIN	16:30:00
1:15 PM	ON10	Box-Doelger	Load	2	12:15 AM	ME-2	11:00:00
1:15 PM	ON10	Box-Iroquois	Load	2	11:59 PM	DE30	10:44:00
1:15 PM	ON10	Diesel Fuel	Load	1	11:59 PM	DE30	10:44:00
1:15 PM	ON10	Propane	Load	1	11:59 PM	DE30	10:44:00
1:15 PM	ON10	Chemicals	Load	2	12:15 AM	ME-2	11:00:00
6:15 PM	ME-2	Box-Doelger	Empty	2	11:59 PM	DE30	5:44:00
6:15 PM	ME-2	Plastics	Empty	2	11:59 PM	DE30	5:44:00
6:15 PM	ME-2	Grain	Empty	4	1:15 AM	SEEL	7:00:00
6:15 PM	ME-2	Chemicals	Empty	2	11:59 PM	DE30	5:44:00
7:45 PM	ELSE	Lumber	Load	3	8:00 AM	ON10	12:15:00
7:45 PM	ELSE	Fayetteville Xfer	Load	1	8:00 AM	ON10	12:15:00
7:45 PM	ELSE	BPA	Load	2	8:00 AM	ON10	12:15:00
7:45 PM	ELSE	Int	n/a	8	5:15 PM	SY1	21:30:00
10:00 PM	DE30	Lumber	Empty	2	4:15 AM	SEIN	6:15:00
10:00 PM	DE30	Fayetteville Xfer	Empty	1	4:15 AM	SEIN	6:15:00
10:00 PM	DE30	Lumber	Empty	1	1:15 AM	SEEL	3:15:00
10:00 PM	DE30	BPA	Empty	2	4:15 AM	SEIN	6:15:00
11:45 PM	ME-2I	Box-Iroquois	Load	4	4:15 AM	SEIN	4:30:00
11:45 PM	ME-2I	Box-Iroquois	Load	2	8:45 PM	ELSE	21:00:00
11:45 PM	ME-2I	Kaolin	Empty	2	8:45 PM	ELSE	21:00:00
11:45 PM	ME-2I	Acid/coal	Empty	2	8:45 PM	ELSE	21:00:00
				93			

4 Jack Trabachino developed an average dwell time chart during the traffic planning for my Onondaga Cutoff layout. Each arriving car on an average day is listed by scheduled arrival, with its planned departure time out and subsequent dwell time. Once your yard is working, these metrics can help yardmasters understand what cars need to be worked first.

fantastically complicated network, even with today's computer systems and automated waybills. In decades past, this was even more complicated, when there were many more railroads and possible routes.

Historically, car movements have been tracked by thousands of railroad employees whose job it is to check car numbers and waybills — a slip of paper accompanying a car that, among other things, dictates the route the car is to take. As we saw in Chapter 3, as each train arrives at a classification yard, its cars are resorted and coupled into a new train which would depart for the next yard — and so on until the car reaches its final customer destination. The cycle endlessly repeats as empty cars are reloaded for new destinations.

On our modeled railroads, car forwarding can be as simple or complicated as we see fit. Some owners enjoy taking cars from their yard and moving them to industry sidings; other owners may have set cars for certain jobs and cars that are routed outbound once they come to the yard from an industry, **5**. This is a fun spot for creativity: modeling the open-ended prototype where cars can be routed across a continent on our closed-loop or end-to-end model railroad. Whatever the system employed, the question we have to address is this: How can we represent the almost infinite variety and interest of the prototype in our very finite modeled operations?

STAGING YARDS AND THE WORLD BEYOND THE LAYOUT

This is where staging yards become so important. The late Allen McClelland, a legendary modeler and pioneer in realistic operations, implored us to think of our modeled operations as a part of a larger network: a link to the rest of the world. The thousands of miles beyond our basement walls are represented through staging: tracks, usually hidden from view, that can hold entire trains before and after they appear on the layout, **6, 7**. This is the "beyond the basement" concept of Allen's well-known HO Virginian & Ohio. Planning for staging is an important exercise to start early in the layout-planning process.

The coming and going of most trains on a layout is included in regular train schedules and therefore in the layout's operations plan. On the prototype, there's an incredible number of variables that can change what and when trains arrive "on scene." Different divisions have different power assignments, blocking assignments, and crew districts, **8**. Any of these can cause delays or changes in sequence. Trains are coming from somewhere and going somewhere else, passing through or stopping in our modeled territory for only a short time as part of their role in the wider transportation network. Representing enough of the variables outside of our modeled territory to capture the variety of prototype operations can be a challenge.

ADEQUATE STAGING

Tony Koester — well-known for his former Allegheny Midland and current Nickel Plate layouts — has a formula for staging that provides a great place to start when planning an operations-based layout. His formula is N = 2n + 1, where the number of staging tracks needed ("N") is equal to two times the number of trains you think you want to run ("n") plus one. This rule can be implemented in different ways depending on the specifics of your track plans and operating goals, and is affected by how your layout is constructed. For example, a key factor is whether your layout is built as a point-to-point railroad with stub-ended staging where operations require turning entire trains, or as a full loop with double-ended staging where each set of equipment turns itself in a loop, **8**. A staging yard can be a dozen or more long tracks on a basement-sized layout or just a pair of short tracks for a small switching layout.

Longtime friend Jack Trabachino was involved with the early concepts and planning for my Onondaga Cutoff (see "A 1990s Layout in an 1840s Basement," *Model Railroad Planning 2018*). We had grown up watching trains together locally in New Jersey, then traveled across the country to do the same. Jack's interests and career path took him to the Rail Service Planning department, the group that plans train schedules, equipment turns, and crew cycles to ensure efficiency. I have been fortunate to be able to tap that experience in both the develop-

5 Lou Steenwyk's model railroad captures iron ore movements from mine to ore dock transload and the return of empties and does it in a grand way. The giant ore yard at Ashland, Wis., is constantly handling ore cars in dedicated service from loadout to transload.

6 Staging is often located on another deck beneath a layout or in another adjacent room. Steve King has his staging yard at Marion, Va., hanging from the ceiling in an adjacent room to his N scale Virginia Midland.

7 Tony Koester's HO Nickel Plate includes stub-ended staging yards at each end of the railroad. Although this requires manual changing of the locomotives and cabooses after each run, it also maximizes the length of each staging track thanks to the lack of a ladder track at the stub end. Rerailers are included to assist in the task of turning the consist.

ment and evolution of the Onondaga Cutoff operating plan, **9**.

My goal was and is to model high-density trunk-line railroading on a double-track, Centralized Traffic Control-equipped main line in the early to mid-1990s. Once we settled on Conrail's Chicago Line in upstate New York as the prototype, we built the Onondaga Cutoff layout to fit the space in my basement. Long trains are the rule on the railroad. This resulted in our designing the OC around and above five long double-ended staging tracks that can each store two trains end to end. Crossovers in the middle of staging tracks 4 and 5 add flexibility, (see page 86). A key feature of this design is that we can use blocks of cars and even entire trains more than once in each operating session — there is no practical way to have 20 to 30 long trains run in a session if we only used each block of cars once. The "magic" of an operating session is that a block of auto racks, for example, can appear on the layout once as an eastbound hotshot, then as the second section of a very large westbound through freight, and then again as a westbound empty train returning to Midwestern auto-assembly plants, all in one session, with only two changes of power — all without detracting from the visual appeal and verisimilitude of the layout's theme. Doing this saves staging space and a great deal of equipment expense.

The overall plausibility of the scheme was quickly evident. The staging yard as installed worked efficiently to handle the traffic and was flexible enough in both access and capacity to handle the ebbs and flows of the operations. In effect, just as actors in a play stay off stage until their cue, staging is where all the trains coming from and going to the world beyond the layout stay until their time to exit stage left or stage right.

Staging is an element of layout design that by its very concept is "gray" compared to other aspects. The visible layout (modeled territory) is what you want viewers and operators to see, and where you emulate the prototype or the vision of the builder and owner. Benchwork, wiring, and control systems are support functions kept "backstage," out of view. Staging yards, on the other hand, are used both to emulate the prototype but also to support the functionality of the visible layout. Your staging yard or yards are therefore one of the most critical elements of your railroad because they provide the bridge between the layout and operations.

Like all aspects of layout construction, staging can be accomplished in many ways. It can be hidden or in plain view and built with full scenery like the rest of the railroad, **10**. It can be in another room or on another level of the layout. It can be stub-ended or double-ended. It can also be simplified as one or two tracks where an operator physically moves trains on and off the tracks to stage them (a "fiddle yard"). All these choices are available for the planner to consider when deciding the type of operation the layout will support.

VISIBLE AND STAGING YARD ARRANGEMENTS

The strategic relationship between visible working yards and staging yards is worthy of a deeper dive. Your planned traffic should come first and will lead to consideration of locations of each, **11**. The traffic patterns will point to options for staging and help to clarify the best possible designs. There are a variety of possibilities; here are a few common options:

Yard or industrial area with staging

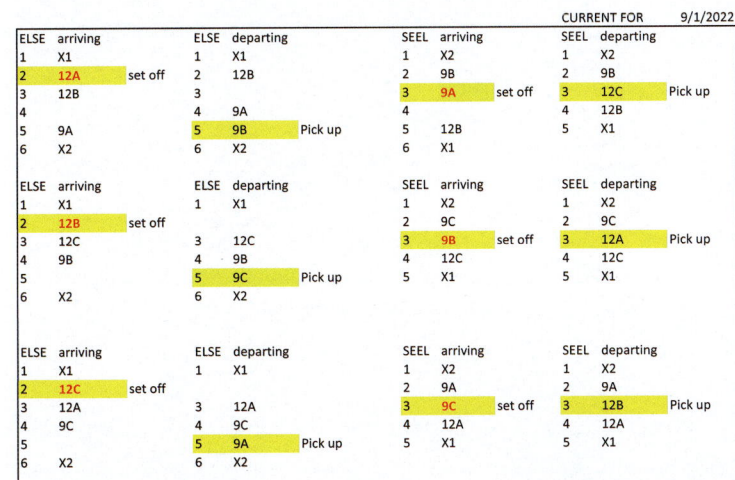

Manifest trains on the Onondaga Cutoff are blocked to accomplish certain car-forwarding goals. At left is the blocking scheme for the trains representing SEEL and ELSE. Others for COSE and SENF are similar. Below: Each block contains a number of cars that are inbound and outbound in certain cycles, which causes them to appear in a consistent pattern much like the prototype. When the blocks are assembled they are moved to a location convenient for pickup.

on either side: This is a classic setup for a switching layout, from a smaller shelf layout to a larger terminal district layout. This sort of approach maximizes switching opportunities, but will come at the expense of any significant main-line running. This option is best used for a branch line or terminal area with limited traffic.

Yard along midpoint of main line, with staging at ends: This setup is more along the lines of many operating model railroads in the hobby today. The focus is on modeling a subdivision or section of main line, with a large yard along the main line between the staging yards, plus a number of towns or industrial switching districts along the route. This is the option we used on the Onondaga Cutoff, **12**.

Yards at each end of main line, with staging beyond both ends: This example encompasses an entire crew district or subdivision and allows for extensive operations with modeled crew changes along a long main line or trunk line route. Having two modeled classification yards, plus the main line, requires a great deal of space.

TYPES OF STAGING YARDS

Given those common styles, let's add another dimension on top of location — the type of staging area.

Stub: This is a single-ended yard, with a series of parallel stub-end tracks each long enough to hold one train. Stub yards maximize capacity, but at the expense of flexibility — every train that enters staging locomotive-first will need to be turned by manually moving the locomotive to the other end of one of the trains. Stub staging is very clear to understand for operations: East is one yard, west is another. It requires

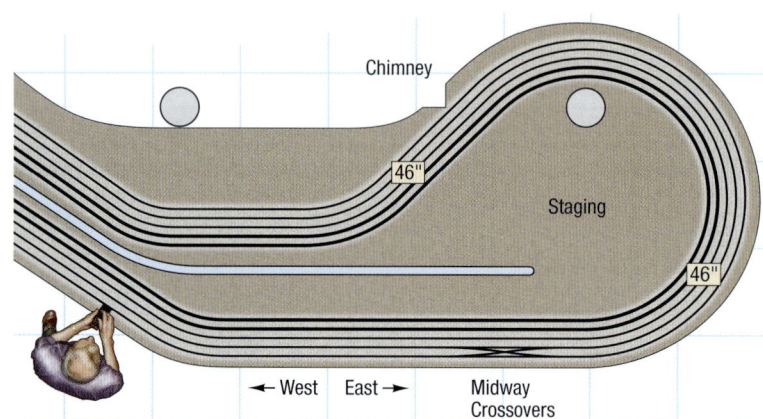

9 Each double-ended staging track on the Onandaga Cutoff holds two trains end-to-end. Above: With Onondaga Yard above, the staging yards representing the main line east and west of the modeled territory are visible below under the glow of simulated sodium-vapor lights. Flexible staging trackage allows for engine changes in staging during sessions, adding to the illusion of a trunk line.

considerable real estate at each end of the run, as well as extensive re-staging between operating sessions, but provides trains that run once and therefore has a potential for great variety during a session.

Through: These are double-ended yards where opposite ends of the main line run into the yard ladder at each end. Having a ladder at each end takes up more space than a stub yard (and shortens the amount of available storage on any track), but the flexibility allows locomotives to be moved under their own power to other trains without the need for extensive re-staging. Further, certain consists can be run with different locomotives later in a session to represent entirely different trains in the schedule, creating an illusion of a busy main line with far less rolling stock needed than would be required for two stub-end staging yards.

Loop: At one or both ends of the main line, staging tracks make a full turn around a "balloon track" to return to the same main track in the opposite direction. Trains are automatically turned when using a loop. Storage tracks are concentric with the main track. Loops take a considerable amount of real estate (especially if you run long cars that require broad minimum-radius curves), and storage tracks are limited by the length in the same manner as the through-style staging yard, but the flexibility and the ability to change locomotives under their own power is again appealing.

Be sure to consider staging early when you design your railroad, as it can be difficult to add staging tracks after a layout is built. Staging yards are critical for what follows: running trains that come from somewhere and go somewhere else. Effective staging makes your railroad more like its prototype.

Staging yards can be visible and scenicked, as this one at West Mesa/East Hill on David Barrow's Cat Mountain & Santa Fe. David Barrow

Staging at the west end of Tony Koester's Nickel Plate layout is on the top level and therefore visible, albeit at a height of more than six feet. Therefore the backdrop and basic scenery are included so as not to detract from the overall atmosphere of the layout space.

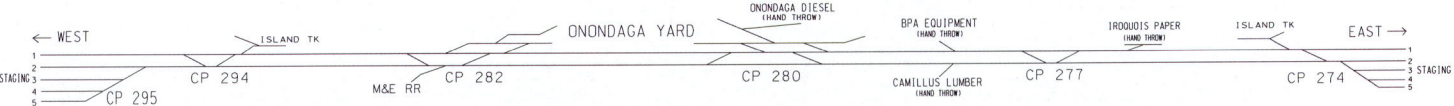

12 As this schematic shows, the layout-design approach for my Onondaga Cutoff was a big yard in the middle of a main line with staging at each end. In my case, that meant a double-ended staging yard common to both ends of the railroad.

CHAPTER EIGHT

MODELING MAINTENANCE AREAS

Railroads are designed to move trains. But "moving" is not a given for giant mechanical devices. Every machine requires maintenance, and on railroads the maintenance for cars and locomotives is quite different. Shop facilities can easily be incorporated into your railroad, **1**. Your yards can also be designed to accommodate maintenance-of-way (MofW) equipment. These features also result in additional locations to spot cars during operating sessions.

1 Angelica, N.Y., on Perry Squier's HO Pittsburg, Shawmut & Northern, includes locomotive maintenance facilities just as the prototype did. Extra No. 70 has arrived, and No. 70 will cut off and be serviced in the shop at left. Old engine No. 8 (far left) has been converted to a stationary boiler to provide power for the shops.

LOCOMOTIVE MAINTENANCE FACILITIES

Every railroad depends on locomotives to move trains. Modelers are universally interested in motive power, and many of us accumulate large collections of locomotives — sometimes in numbers beyond what we need (or can even fit on our layouts). To make these locomotive models effectively work for us, we need to step back and see the larger picture.

The most locomotive-intensive real estate on any railroad is the locomotive servicing facility. How do these function, what do they do, and how can we best model them? Motive-power infrastructure (which includes shop buildings, turntables and roundhouses, fueling stations (coal, oil, or diesel fuel, depending upon era), sanding towers, and other ancillary structures and equipment) is expensive in dollars, real estate, and labor, and represents a huge investment by a railroad. This investment is only justified by keeping locomotives ready to move.

On small railroads that have just one or a few locomotives, the plan is simple: maintain the locomotive when the train isn't running so that the crew can use the locomotive when the train is running. A spur track, perhaps with a simple single locomotive-sized shed, can serve as the de facto engine facility, **2**.

For larger railroads, though, managing motive power quickly takes on a new level of complexity. Mid-sized and major railroads have fleets of locomotives to keep in good repair. In the steam era, locomotives required extensive routine maintenance and followed a logical series of steps upon arrival at a yard. They cut away from their train and made their way to the engine facility, **3**. A hostler took control and filled the tender with coal (or oil) and water. He also filled the sandbox, then moved the engine to a pit to dump ashes from firebox, **4**. Minor repairs and and lubrication would be done; if more substantial repairs were needed, it would go to the roundhouse, **5**, **6**. Once the engine was ready to go, a hostler would move it to a ready track for assignment to an outbound train, **7**.

On the Onondaga Cutoff, the Minoa & Euclid (M&E) is a shortline railroad operating over former Lackawanna trackage to an interchange with Conrail at Onondaga Yard. Morristown & Erie is the parent company of the M&E and supplies locomotives for this operation. Here, Nos. 17 and 19 are at the small locomotive facility at Euclid Yard.

Ashland & Iron River No. 45, a 2-8-2 Mikado, has cut away from the long string of empty ore jennies en route back to the mines and heads for the servicing area and roundhouse at Bessemer, Mich. Operations on Lou Steenwyk's railroad focus on iron ore but include the mix of traffic common to the Iron Range in this era.

Diesel facilities, like their steam-era predecessors, adhere to regular routines to service locomotives. Diesels, however, can travel much farther between fueling and service (and require less daily maintenance) compared to steam. This means diesels often run through division points and crew-change points where steam locomotives were once changed. (Many division-point yards lost their engine facilities for this reason.) There are federal requirements for certain levels of inspection and maintenance that must be done based on days in service.

With diesels, inbound locomotives are brought into the facility by a crew. A hostler will move the locomotive

89

4 Steam locomotives created quite a bit of coal ash. Here Maumee No. 521 is spotted at the ash pit at Dacron on Bill Darnaby's HO Maumee Route. Next stop is the water column at left. Bill Darnaby

5 Perry Squier created a town, yard, and engine facility for operations at Olean, N.Y., on his HO Pittsburg, Shawmut & Northern. Perry Squier

through the various parts of the facility to ensure all required inspection and maintenance occurs in proper order. From service and inspection (S&I) tracks and bays to the fuel rack and then to the ready track, locomotives are moved through the stages of preparation for another run. Each one is given a visual inspection, ensuring the mandated inspections are up to date, **8**. Paperwork is verified and the locomotive is moved to refill fuel and sand. Water and oil are checked, cab interiors are cleaned, retention toilets emptied, and windows and lights wiped down. Engines are then moved to a ready track.

Another option for diesel-era railroads is to include mainline refueling stations where road trains pull up to a fuel station built right alongside the main line. This enables refueling without having to uncouple or swap locomotives, and is common at key points on busy railroads, **9**. This is a great way to scenic a visible staging yard!

All of this activity is an exciting part of a yard scene and can be tailored to fit the needs of your layout. A few key layout design elements help visitors feel like they are part of the scene. First, allowing enough space in an aisle so that viewers can pause along the enginehouse scenes is important. Locating the enginehouse toward the middle or even front of the scene, close to the aisle, puts crew members and viewers "on the property," **10**.

This process of moving locomotives around the facility to duplicate prototype operations also provides opportunities to appreciate the models' details and weathering and to make photographs that evoke the same mystique as shop photos on the prototype, **11,**

6 The turntable control panel at Frankfort is easily accessible from the aisle, left, which allows the hostler to make quicker moves. Toggles throw turnouts, while buttons turn power on for the tracks where locomotives are stored. Right: Tony cleverly disguised the view of the control panel with two walls of a brick shop building at Frankfort.

Thurmond, Va., has a small yard and engine facility right on the main line as modeled by Ted Pamperin. The limited space between the river and mountain meant restricted ready tracks and a great modeled scene. Ted Pamperin

Locomotives congregate at the diesel shop at Union Pacific's J.R. Davis Yard in Roseville, Calif., on March 15, 2010. Five tracks run through the shop building. The shop performs a variety of mechanical inspections and maintenance.

Mainline fuel racks ("fueling pads") exist to allow quick refueling of locomotives while on trains. Here Union Pacific workers at Las Vegas, Nev., refuel UP SD40-2 3795 and sisters on an eastbound freight on Oct. 4, 1985. Al Tillotson

My Onondaga Yard has a busy engine facility. Blue flags, like the one hanging from the handrail on CR 1931, indicate that mechanical workers may be working on the equipment — don't move it until the flag is removed!

12. Large open doors and windows on roundhouses and other shop buildings can allow for creative photography. By placing the camera low to include some of the interior of the facility in the image, the resulting photo can feel like you're standing in your layout's shop doors. We can include some basic details in the interior that help draw attention and add to the flavor of what we are trying to capture. For additional detailed information on the specifics of modeling engine facilities and their operations, see Tony Koester's book *Steam and Diesel Locomotive Servicing Terminals* (published by Kalmbach).

CAR SHOPS

Except for the smallest shortline railroads, maintenance facilities for railcars are separate from those used for locomotives. For your railroad, this may include a paved or unpaved track or two with jacks, a small crane, spare parts, and wheelsets, **13, 14**. Today, federal standards exist for wheel and brake wear, as well as air brake systems, steps, grab irons, and other equipment. These wear and are damaged occasionally during regular use and repairs are made as needed. Railroads for generations have called these RIP (repair-in-place) tracks, **15**. In our modeled yards, RIP tracks provide another location to set out cars, and they can be interesting scenes — they're great locations to stage old freight cars or trailers as storage (perhaps you have a nicely weathered car that doesn't run well), **16**.

With larger yards come larger numbers of cars, and their needs are more efficiently met with better and bigger facilities. Many mid- and large-size freight yards include dedicated buildings or — especially in the South — open-air roofed areas where workers can perform major repairs or rebuilding out of the elements. Into the 2020s, many shops formerly owned by railroads have been sold to contractors for use as for-hire shops, where railroads and private car owners can have cars repaired, repainted, or fully rebuilt.

Some railroads were large enough to commission entire industrial complexes to construct and maintain a vast fleets of freight cars. It comes as no surprise that the Pennsylvania Railroad had vast facilities world-renowned in the day including its Juniata Shops, **17**, and the Samuel Rea Car Shops in Altoona, Pa., and Hollidaysburg, Pa., respectively. Juniata is still the main

Locomotives line the S&I (service and inspection) tracks at Onondaga Yard, which hold a collection of Conrail locomotives for local and road service. Detailing inside structures will be apparent through large windows.

Yard tracks where equipment pauses make for a great place to examine the details modelers add to the equipment. Conrail GE C30-7A 6577 is a kitbash of a locomotive unique to Conrail that was very common on the modeled territory of the Onondaga Cutoff.

locomotive shop for Norfolk Southern, while the Samuel Rea shops (named after the president of the PRR from 1913 to 1925) are owned by a private car rebuilder, Curry Rail Services.

PASSENGER CAR SERVICING

Passenger cars share some basic maintenance practices with freight cars but are considerably more complex and require specialized services. Federal requirements for maintenance are stringent for safety. Passenger cars need daily inspections, **18**. Water tanks need to be refilled, wastewater tanks drained, restrooms and interior surfaces cleaned, and heating and air conditioning filters changed. Sleepers and diners require linen changing and restocking of supplies.

Steam and transition-era passenger facilities were complex, as the number of passenger trains was much larger than from the 1960s through today. On any railroad of substantial size, passenger yards could serve hundreds of cars ranging from simple coaches to diners, kitchen cars, observation, and club cars, all of which had their own service needs, **19**. Pullman service was another fascinating complexity with cars requiring cleaning and linen supplies before night runs. Baggage, express, and mail service had their own service requirements and facilities.

APPLYING IDEAS TO MODEL RAILROADS

Maintenance is extremely important to prototype railroads. Railroads go to great lengths to avoid over-the-road failures, and they invest significant assets, labor, and real estate to perform scheduled inspections, lubrication, and maintenance of equipment to keep it running smoothly.

Our model railroads should work to accomplish the same thing. Allow some space, however minimal, to suggest maintenance operations. Even just a simple side track in your yard with repair trucks, jacks, and supplies (and workers) takes only a few inches of space and can even function as another "industry" to be switched. Modeling maintenance is a great way to ensure a yard looks like it is meeting the needs of your railroad.

13 Car shops are common at many yards, and more substantial yards have more infrastructure dedicated to car maintenance and repair. A line of Shawmut boxcars rest at the car shop at St. Marys, Pa., on Perry Squier's model railroad. Rolling stock in the early wood-car era required more maintenance than later steel cars.

14 St. Marys also has a passenger car shop, with an old boxcar that has been repurposed as a shed. Scenes like this add a lot of personality to a yard scene.

Colorado & Southern boxcar No. 7893 was set out for minor repairs at the Seventh Street Yard's RIP (repair-in-place) track on Doug Tagsold's layout. Crews had reported that the boxcar's brakes were failing to release properly. Many yards have these tracks where crews make minor repairs to freight cars. Doug Tagsold

Old equipment adds character to many scenes, and yards are a natural gathering place for it. Here the RIP (repair-in-place) tracks at Onondaga Yard include an old piggyback trailer from Conrail predecessor Erie Lackawanna, which is now being used as a supply shed.

17 The massive Juniata Shops at Altoona, Pa., were built by the Pennsylvania Railroad and remained the main shops of Conrail. Today they are Norfolk Southern's main shop location and include storage and repair tracks for cars as well. This image from 2005 shows the turntable area, which is still in daily use in 2023.

18 The Spadina coach yard in Toronto, Ont., was home to a fleet of passenger equipment. Access doors are open for maintenance on a former Reading dining car lettered for Canadian National and now working for VIA Rail Canada. Rich Taylor

19 Canadian National's Spadina coach yard was located in downtown Toronto, a major passenger hub, where it served Toronto Union Station. It was responsible for storing cars between runs and assembling trains as well as daily maintenance and extensive repairs. Rich Taylor

CHAPTER NINE

1 Day or night, yards are working, and the yardmaster is the person that sets the goals and communicates how to get there. Sunrise is on the horizon as YAON-20, the overnight yard job at Onondaga Yard, finishes his work.

THE YARDMASTER: SETTING THE PACE

"OK, up to the yard office, give the yardmaster a call." The phrase has been used on nearly every railroad at one point or another, and in the end — despite all the history, planning, and design, regardless of construction or use or capacity — railroading comes down to people. A yard is no more (and no less) than the people who operate it. And those people need a common goal and base of communication, **1**. Central to this is one of the most important (and fun!) operational positions on any model railroad: the yardmaster.

As we've emphasized, yards exist to classify and sort cars into outbound trains destined for other locations or for local delivery. The yardmaster is the person with the clear role of making that movement happen in an organized manner, and having fun while doing it, **2**. There are other titles, depending on the size of the operation and the intensity of the use and nature of the given yard, and different railroads varied in their methods of organizing management. For our purposes, "yardmaster" means the person in charge of a yard area, the manager who directs the team of individuals ranging from assistant yardmasters to switching crews and car inspectors, to handle the traffic.

The late Andy Sperandeo, a noted model railroader and veteran yardmaster, offered much insight over the years on his philosophy on handling yards in his monthly "The Operators" column in *Model Railroader*, including

Model Railroader editor Eric White works as yardmaster at Glenwood Yard on John Goodhart's Lake Erie, Cincinnati & St. Louis Railroad. Having a dedicated operator's space that allows yard personnel to stand clear of an aisle helps to keep traffic moving.

CONRAIL ONONDAGA CUTOFF — SEPTEMBER 24 1994, rev 8-10

Time	at	FROM Staging	SYMBOL East	West	DISP. Staging	Next Train East	West	Power	Departure Notes	Arrival Notes	Power Relay
0900	CP282 1000		ME-1		ME YD				LIGHT TO IROQUOIS	WORK & RETURN LIGHT TO EUCLID	
0900	CP294	1W	NFSE			1E	ON10 ML401	6577-6860-6639-6482	TRACK 1 @ CP 277	STOP WHEN HIND END CLEARS CP 274 POWER TO ISL STUB ON ARRIVAL FOR UBO24A	UBO24A
0930	CP274	4E		TV77	5W	TV24		6075-6495-6155		HOLD FOR TV200 ARRIVAL	TV202
0955	CP294	4W	TV200		4E	TV202		6026-6789-6611		4W-ISL 7 ON ARRIVAL TV77 POWER COUPLE 5W-4E, ADV TO CP295	
1015	CP274	1E			ON10 14 CARS	ON YD		1989-1987	IROQUOIS: S/O CARS 1-6, P/U 2		
1100	CP294	5W	TV24		4E-MID-4W		TV13	6019-6807		HOLD FOR TV13 DEPARTURE	TV261
1130	CP274	2E			SY1 18 CARS	ON YD	SY1	NYSW3006-3612-3636			
1145	CP274	5E		TV79	5W	TV14		5046-5004-3327-3382		CUT OFF TO 5E, HOLD FOR TV202 DEPARTURE	TV10
1215	CP294	2W	BRSE		2	SLSE		6286-BN7081-BN6353		ISL EXP ON ARRIVAL	
1300	CP294	3W	A276		3E	A273EQ		AMTK 227		HOLD EQ FOR ML401 DEP., TV13 DISPOSITION	
1305	CP274	4E		TV13	1W-1E	TV9		6712-ATSF5140-5076	TV24 4W-4E-ISL 7	HOLD FOR ML401 DEPARTURE	
1325	CP294	4W	TV202		5E-5W	TV556		6155-6495-6075	TV79 5E-4W-ISL CONN	FOLLOW TV14 TO CP295 POWER TO ISL EXP ON ARRIVAL	
1345	CP274	1E		ML401	4W		ML403	3312-6453-6462	TV13 ADV CP274 W/ TRAIN, TO LAYOFF W/ STACKS A276 REV 3E-LAYOFF. CUT ENGINE TO ISL EXP	CUT OFF TO 5E HOLD FOR TV556 DEPARTURE	SLSE
1420	CP294	5W	TV14		4E	TVLA		5088-6437-5025		COUPLE 4E-4W	ML403
1455	CP274	1E		TV9	1W-1E	TV99		5056-5031-5054		ISL S&I 2 ON ARRIVAL	
1525	CP274	5W	TV556		2E	TV261		SSW8057-SP8028-SP9730	ML401 RELAY 5E-5W-2W	HOLD FOR TV261 DEPARTURE	
1540	CP274	4E		TVLA	1W-1E	TV100		5544-6416-6852	A273 94LD-5W-4E WHEN AVAILABLE	HOLD FOR ELSE DEPARTURE	ML480
1605	CP274	1E		TV99	1W	TV10		6039-6000	UBO24A 74LD-5E-5W WHEN AVAILABLE	COUPLE AHEAD	TV100
1620	CP294	3W	NPSE		3	ELSE		UP6218-UP9100-UP5017		ISL S&I 2 ON ARRIVAL	
1530 1700	ON YD CP280	SR	SY1 20 CARS		5E-5W		SYBU	3636-3612-3006		ADV TO CP295. HOLD ON TRAIN	
1645	CP282 1705		ME-2		ME YD				8 CARS ONONDAGA	RETURN TO EUCLID FROM ONONDAGA	
1600 1705	94LD CP274	5W-4E			A273	1W		AMTK 488	ADV ML403 4W-4E	STOP WHEN CLEAR OF CP295 REV TRAIN TO ISL LAYOFF	
1620 1710	74LD CP294	5E-5W	UBO-24A		5E-5W			6482-6639-6860-6577	HOLD @ CP274 UNTIL A273 CLEAR MIDWAY	HOLD OR CUT @ MIDWAY FOR ML403 POWER IF SY1 AHEAD HOLD ON TRAIN FINISH	
1730	CP274	2E		TV261	4W-4E	ML480		6807-6019	TV556 REV 2E-ISL 9	ISL S&I 1 ON ARRIVAL	
1755	CP274	4E		ML403	4W	ML480		5025-6437-5088		RELAY 5W - TIE DOWN	
1830	CP282	3	ELSE 45 CARS		3		SEIN	702-6001-6666-8045	S/O BLOCK 2; P/U BEHIND BLOCK 4 TVLA RELAY 1E-3E-3W-4W	HOLD ON TRAIN FINISH	
1905	CP294	2W	SLSE		2		SENF	6462-6453-3312		HOLD ON TRAIN FINISH DE30 RAR-2E	
1945	CP294	4W+4E	ML480		4E-4W	ML482 TV8W		6852-6416-5544		CUT STACKS AT MIDWAY 4E; ADV TO 4W CP295 HOLD ON TRAIN FINISH	
2025	CP294	1W	TV10		1E-1W	TV6		3382-3327-5004-5046	TRACK 1 @ CP 277	HOLD ON TRAIN FINISH	
2030	CP274	2E			DE30 5 CARS	ON Yd		1967-CN9549	DO NOT USE TRACK 1 @ CP274 PICKUP ME1 OUTBOUNDS AT IROQUOIS	SWAP WITH ENGINEHOUSE	
2045	CP294	1E-1W	TV100			1E	TV7	6000-6039	TRACK 1 @ CP 277	HOLD ON TRAIN FINISH	

A lineup of the trains that are coming next is critical to prioritize yard movements and keep things fluid. On the Onondaga Cutoff, the lineup is provided ahead of time; gray shading indicates trains originating or terminating at Onondaga while red indicates trains that work the yard.

3

Good communication and empty yard tracks get a smile out of veteran OC yardmaster Tillotson.

Clovis yardmaster Jay Hastings has a short block for St. Louis routed back to an empty track that will build a new outbound Q-CVLI train on Sammy Carlisle's Santa Fe Hereford Sub layout. He's smiling as he's ahead of the curve: two more intermodal trains will be along within the next few hours, each with a block of cars for St. Louis. The train will be powered and depart Clovis before running east to staging.

The ability to see what the next outbound block is going to be, and the block after that, is critical. The yardmaster needs a lineup of which trains are due in and out, **3**. Thinking ahead ensures that the next outbounds are sorted and ready for picking up before their train arrives. What if it turns out you need to handle a car three or four times to make that happen? Well, you go forward and do what it takes. Ideally every car should be handled a minimum number of times, but even more important is that the yard keeps moving so the next cut of outbounds is ready. Operating a yard is fun because it emulates the urgency of prototype operations, **4**. Doing nothing is not really an option for long in railroading. In fact, doing nothing is always the wrong thing, as the system will then quickly break down.

Early in my career, a close friend and colleague of mine was sitting quietly at his desk at headquarters and a senior executive poked his head in as he walked by. "Hey — look, do something. Anything! Even if it's wrong." He then walked out. It turns out it's an old adage in rail operations: better to have action, even inefficient action, than no action at all. Making decisions is how we learn to make good decisions and avoid inefficient action.

Decision-making is a natural process for some but for others it is a learned process. No matter which you are, you can still handle a job as a yardmaster. It just requires some basics that Andy mentions. The key is to consider and then to act. Make the best decision you can in the moment and move on. Action on a railroad is continuous and the clock doesn't stop. The 24-hour nature of railroading means that mistakes and delays can pile up and compound. It may seem overwhelming, but in practice we just take it step by step. Here are a few key points to keep in mind:

• **Keep a track open** for incoming moves, **5**. Yards with no open tracks get tied up quickly — even more so in modeled yards due to the space constraints we deal with. If you have more outbound blocks than you have tracks in the yard, you will need to double

the one reprinted on page 99. Note in it the assumption that there is a person running the decision making — Andy, in writing this short piece, is acting as a yardmaster. He would be advising trains the same way he writes the sentences: the track on which to leave or pick up a block of cars, which track to use to run around, when to move and depart. Yardmasters (really, managers anywhere on the railroad) are there to make decisions.

A telltale sign of success in a yard is a yardmaster who is thinking ahead.

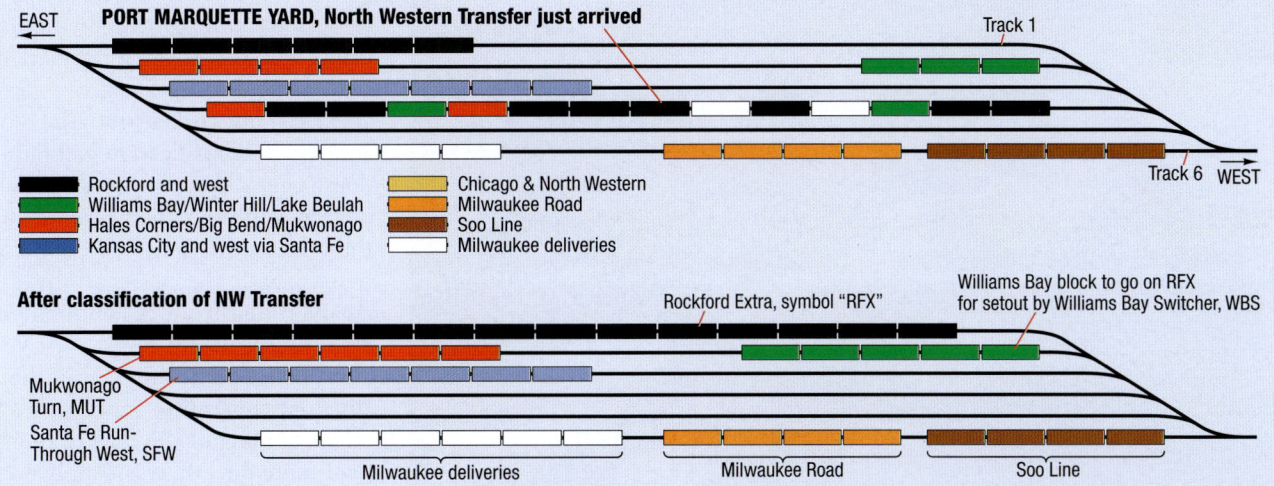

WORKING YARDS

// By Andy Sperandeo *From Model Railroader, May 2007*

I'm almost always willing to take on a freight yard job when I'm invited to an operating session. It really doesn't matter if I've even seen the layout before or know anything about its operating patterns — I'm happy to do it. Am I just foolhardy and overconfident?

Quite possibly. However, I've also learned through experience and observation how yards are supposed to work, and I know they all pretty much work the same way.

The basic function of any freight yard is what the railroads call "classification." That's sorting cars with similar routings or destinations together to build trains, or blocks for trains carrying cars with multiple destinations. Each grouping is a "classification," and you "classify" cars by sorting them.

For efficiency, the classification needs to be done as cars arrive in the yard, so trains are ready before they're supposed to leave.

Port Marquette Yard. I can illustrate classification switching with an actual example instead of something abstract. The diagrams above show Port Marquette Yard, the Milwaukee freight terminal on our old HO scale Milwaukee, Racine & Troy club layout. The colored blocks represent cars, and the key shows the classifications represented by each color. Notice that we had eight classifications but only six tracks in the yard. Some doubling up was necessary, especially since the yard crew kept at least one track clear for arriving trains. Having more classifications than tracks is typical of model railroad yards.

In the upper diagram, track four is occupied by cars with a variety of destinations just brought in by a transfer from the Chicago & North Western. The next assignment for the two Port Marquette switchers, one working from either end, is to classify the cars from the North Western and add them to the blocks already standing in the yard.

(There are no cars in Port Marquette for the C&NW because the transfer job took them back to its base in Butler, Wis., represented by a staging track to the east.)

Classification builds trains. The lower diagram shows the yard after the cars from the North Western have been classified. As you can see, they've gone directly into blocks being built for outbound trains, as identified in the lower diagram.

The RFX and SFW are both through trains headed west. The WBS and MUT blocks on track two are both for way freights, but they'll be handled differently. The WBS block will go out on the head end of the RFX, and that train will set out those cars at Williams Bay for a road switcher based there. The MUT operates as a turn to its namesake station and back, and it'll be clear to pull to the west out of track two once the RFX departs with the WBS block.

The cars on six are in three blocks. The Soo cars are at the west end for pickup by a westbound Soo train operating over the MR&T on trackage rights. After a few more Milwaukee Road cars show up in arriving trains, the yard crew will pull the middle block off six and start building a transfer for that connection on track four or five. When there's a lull in the yard switching, the east end switcher will spot the Milwaukee deliveries at local industries, returning to the yard with pickups to be classified.

Where to next? And so it went. The yard was always in a state of flux as trains came and left, but the outbound trains were usually ready in plenty of time for scheduled departures because we classified the incoming cars upon arrival.

I haven't said anything about our car-routing system. We had one, but its particulars don't matter. As long as the paperwork in your operating system indicates where cars arriving at a yard are going next, you'll have the essential information needed for efficient classification switching.

one or two of them onto tracks to allow that open track to exist. It's OK to push back in tight times and have trains hold out — get a track open first, then allow the work.

• **First out comes first.** The best strategy for classification will fail if it doesn't get the next upcoming block out efficiently. So, the first block or train due out is your first job. Build it and handle the others afterwards. Again, if that requires handling cars an extra time, so be it.

• **Have a plan.** Inherent in the "first out comes first" strategy is a clear understanding of the flow of trains. Said more directly, it is simply not feasible to manage a yard without a list of trains due in and out. On the other hand, while it is important to have a plan, the yardmaster has to be flexible enough to junk that plan when and as needed. Railroad life, even in miniature, doesn't always hap-

6 Bob Tegtmeier has brought his coal train into Vals Creek Yard on Steve King's Virginia Midland N scale railroad. Experienced yardmaster Henry Freeman works with him to sort paperwork and make a setout. Communication is key to keep a yard moving.

7 The Conrail Mohawk Dispatcher, Chris Lee, sits next to trainmaster Rich Wisneski during operations on the Onondaga Cutoff. The Mohawk dispatcher has a dedicated telephone to the yardmaster at Onondaga Yard, which helps managers coordinate moves without tying up radio channels. The "hotline" telephone is an indispensable tool for operations and also adds a fun 1990s prototype flavor.

pen as we intend. Trains get delayed, people misread directions, equipment malfunctions, and dispatchers have their own seemingly capricious ideas so that trains sometimes arrive out of order compared to the train list. At that point, you'll need to improvise, but changing the plan only works when you had a plan to start with.

• **Communicate.** Railroad yards are rarely a one-person operation. Even if you only have one dedicated yardmaster who also performs switching duties, incoming and departing road crews effectively become part of the yard team until their trains are "put to bed" or depart yard limits, **6**. Often the single most difficult job for yardmasters is effective communication. Yard crews need to work together to switch blocks and cars; road crews need to know what is expected of them at all times.

Communication is worth a deeper dive. Over time, railroads have adapted all sorts of communications technology to assist operations. Standard whistle and hand signals, lineside signals, flags, lights, waybills and switch lists have all come in due time. Timetables and subsequent train orders helped make main lines fluid and provided a safe, consistent and rule-driven path to keep trains moving when delays happen. But train orders aren't much help inside yard limits.

The advent of radios added tremendously to efficiency and safety on main lines, but more importantly (from the perspective of the yardmaster) also in the yards. Moving cars in yards with radio communication allows for far safer and more efficient moves.

SWITCH LISTS AND CAR CARDS

Waybills on the prototype are the paper documents that follow cars across the railroad. It's how railroads track what cars go where. Among other information, the waybill lists the car's reporting marks and number, load description, originating location, destination, and preferred routing. Modelers generally duplicate this feature with "car cards," simplified small cards that include basic information needed by crews (reporting marks, number, destination).

Under direction of yardmaster Al Tillotson, Conrail freight SEEL (Selkirk, N.Y. to Elkhart, Ind.) makes a reverse move to couple to a pickup. Conductor Ralph Heiss is on the leading end of the reverse movement and uses the radio to communicate with his engineer.

See page 102 for details.

The switch list is developed from waybills of a cut of cars or of a full train. It's a list of basic information (reporting marks, number, destination) and helps operators visualize what cars need to go where. It can be handwritten based on waybills; modern railroads generate lists automatically by computer. The switch list is a key to successful communication between a yardmaster and his crews. It provides a clear direction for each car and block and provides a logical sequence for a yard crew to set up outbound blocks and trains in order. This works for our modeled railroads, too.

From an operations perspective, well-constructed switch lists allow yard crews to determine the best way to get cars sorted while allowing the yardmaster to attend to the myriad other tasks that fall on his or her plate. Trust between the yardmaster and crews builds quickly when they are working well together, with everyone's goals clearly outlined.

Another important aspect is the communication between yardmaster and the dispatcher. While the dispatcher is not in charge of movements within the yard, the dispatcher has the ability to provide an overview of mainline traffic and can help the yardmaster to "peek down the road" to know what is coming next — vital especially if there are delays or changes to the schedule. For most of the history of railroading, this is where the telephone has proved crucial. By 1880, the earliest examples of railroad telephones were in use and by 1900 most railroad dispatchers on the larger roads had open "party" or "block" lines. As soon as dedicated lines were feasible, communication directly between yards and the dispatcher was established.

For your modeled yard, consider adding a dedicated communication line like the prototype did. This can be as simple as an FRS (family radio service) two-way radio or walkie-talkie or, ideally, a closed-circuit telephone line such as those available from Model Railroad Control Systems (www.modelrailroadcontrolsystems.com/telephone/). The goal is to give the yardmaster a priority line to the dispatcher and vice versa, **7**. This can greatly add a prototype feel to communication, **8**.

In the end, remember that yards flux and flow. A good way to see this in total is to view a case study, and the sidebar on page 104 provides a good one from an experienced yardmaster who's also a great teacher. Al Tillotson is one of the veterans on my Onondaga Cutoff operating crew. He's our best yardmaster, and he will close this chapter with a walk-through of a full modeled 24 hours at Onondaga Yard (see page 104).

CAR CARDS AND SWITCH LISTS

// By Andy Sperandeo From *The Model Railroader's Guide to Freight Yards*

The car-card-and-waybill system for directing freight car movements consists of three elements: a car card for each car on the railroad, at least one four-step waybill card for each car, and file boxes for organizing the cards at yards, stations, and other industrial areas.

One of the most commonly used car cards is a 2" x 4" card printed with blank lines for the car information. The bottom third of the card folds up and is taped on each side to form a pocket for the waybill card.

Waybills are printed with four numbered steps, one each on the top and bottom of each side. When placed in the pocket of the car card, only the facing top step shows, and that represents the car's next destination. If the car is already at that location, it remains until the waybill is turned to show the next destination or step. When a car has been to all four destinations indicated by the waybill, there are two options: the waybill can be removed and replaced with another waybill for that type of car or it can simply be turned to show its first step again and repeat the cycle indefinitely.

The first model railroaders to use car-card-and-waybill systems usually had file boxes at each station with three pockets labeled "set out," "hold," and "pick up." By cycling cards through these pockets, they kept cars at their spots for at least one operating session to simulate loading or unloading time. A disadvantage of this procedure was that train crews had to turn the waybill cards and advance the car cards from pocket to pocket.

Now it's more popular to simply provide a box for each industry track or car spot. The layout host turns the waybills as needed or desired between operating sessions, and train crews simply pick up cars with waybills showing another destination and leave those that indicate their present location.

For yards it's always best to have a file pocket for each yard track. The car cards are kept in the same order as the cars stand on the track so they can be used as a switch list for sorting and train makeup. Taller "blocking" cards can be used at the back of the pockets to show classification assignments. These cards can also carry the blocking instructions for their respective trains for easy reference. As an alternative, some operators use magnetic tags to show track assignments.

Printed car cards, waybills, and three-pocket wooden bill boxes like the ones shown are available from Micro-Mark (www.micromark.com). The starter set is no. 82916, and additional cards, waybills, and bill boxes are also available. Software for printing your own car cards and waybills is available as part of the Java Model Railroad Interface (JMRI) software, jmri.org.

Here are examples of a completed car card (left) and a folded and taped blank card (right). I used the "DESC." line to indicate the Santa Fe car class, but it could also be used for the car color or other descriptive information.

A blank waybill form is shown at the right, with a filled-out waybill shown in the car card for boxcar 129624 at left. In this case the car is consigned empty for loading on the Great Northern and routed by way of the Santa Fe's connection with the Western Pacific at Stockton, Calif. The waybill can have as much or as little information as you care to provide, but where the car is going and perhaps how it will get there are about the minimum requirements. On my model railroad this would take the car off the layout into staging representing lines to the north and east.

When the car comes back to the Santa Fe, it's carrying a load of shook wood (the lumber used to make fruit-packing crates) consigned to a packinghouse in Riverside, Calif. This information allows San Bernardino yard crews to block it into a local freight that will head into staging representing lines to the west and south.

Empty again, the Santa Fe boxcar is heading back north for another load.

Once more car 129624 is back with a load of shook wood, but this time it's consigned to a packer on the coast southeast of Los Angeles. This time the yard will classify it into symbol freight SDX bound for San Diego, a destination also represented by staging.

Two Micro-Mark bill boxes placed side by side provide enough pockets for this small yard. I labeled them for each numbered track, plus the drill track and the icing track. The track 2 through 4 pockets each have a yellow blocking card at the back; unused blocking cards are stored in the drill track box. I made the red card in the track 1 pocket for a caboose, and I also made blue "ice" tickets for the reefers in the icing track. After the cars have been spotted for sufficient time, the ice tickets can be pulled and the cars sent on to the destinations on their waybills.

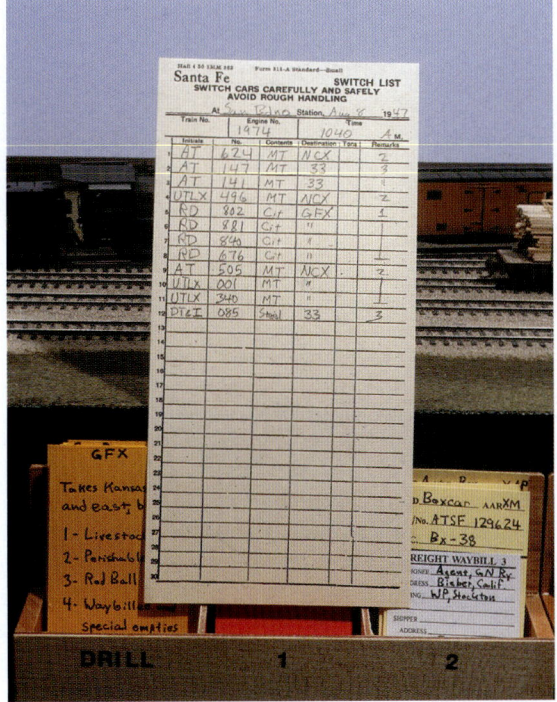

Here's an example of a switch list made out according to the car-card information and waybill instructions. The cars are listed in the order they stand on the track. The switcher will pull the track and sort the cars according to the list. Deciphering the entries is easy: line 1 means the AT&SF ("AT") car with the last three digits "624" is an empty leaving our yard on train NCX (Northern California Express), and the foreman wants it on track 2. Line 4 is a UTLX (Union Tank Line) car with the last three digits "496" also leaving on the NCX, so it's also going to track 2. Line 8 is an SFRD ("RD") refrigerator car, last three digits "676," loaded with citrus fruit. It will go out on the "Green Fruit Express," train GFX, which the crew is building on track 1. The list can be written out quickly, and then all the switching is done without further handling.

24 HOURS AT ONONDAGA YARD

// By Al Tillotson

To give a sense of how freight yards work, let's look at a typical 24 hours at Onondaga Yard on Dave Abeles' Conrail Onondaga Cutoff. Normally Dave's operating sessions cover 12 scale hours (four real-time hours using a 3:1 fast clock), so this description represents two complete operating sessions. We'll begin our day at 6 a.m. (0600 on the fast clock), first following the day yard crew YAON14 (Yard, Albany division, ONondaga yard, 14, or ON14 for short), then later the night switcher YAON20, which comes on duty at 1800 (6 p.m.).

From west (left) to east (right), Onondaga Yard starts at CP 282 (Control Point at milepost 282, controlled by the Mohawk division dispatcher) and is bounded to the north by the North Running Track (known as the North Runner) and to the south by the South Runner as far as CP 280, where a switching lead known as the East Lead continues eastward (through the interlocking) to a stub track under the road bridge. The Onondaga Cutoff main tracks parallel the yard to the south. (See the diagram on page 106.)

Getting an early start seven days a week is Conrail yard job YAON-14, which quickly goes to work each morning classifying cars at Onondaga Yard.

N.Y.) on the South Runner to be worked. There are 10 cars to be classified: four for interchange to New York, Susquehanna & Western's SY1; five paper mill cars bound for interchange to Minoa & Eastern train ME1; and one car for the M&E heading to Euclid, N.Y. ON14 quickly puts these cars to bed in the Field and Park yards.

Simultaneously, the locomotives for local freight WAON10 (Wayfreight/local, Albany Division, ONondaga yard) emerge from the engine servicing area and proceed to the east end of seven cars on a track in the Park Yard. After coupling on and doing a brake test, ON10 departs eastward through CP 280.

Around 0700, ON14 will take advantage of a lull in activity in the yard and take four cars out of the Park Yard for local delivery on the Cazenovia Industrial Track, which connects at the east end of Onondaga Yard. There is a large Blue Circle Cement plant on the industrial track, as well as a scrap dealer, and ON14 will spend a couple of hours working those industries.

At 0930, Minoa & Euclid's ME1 with two cars is on its line that connects with the Onondaga Cutoff at CP 282, asking for permission into the yard. He'll be dropping those two cars for later pickup by Conrail road train ELSE on an empty track in the Park Yard, then picking up seven cars from an adjacent track to forward east to the Iroquois Paper Mill, about four miles beyond CP 280, where M&E's ME3 job handles contract in-plant switching.

By 1000, ME1 is on its way eastward as ON14 returns from the Cazenovia with four cars: two for Massena, N.Y., via WAON10 and two that will eventually head out on WADE30 to Dewitt Yard in East Syracuse. These are put away in the Park Yard; ON14 then ties up in the clear for a coffee break.

At 1030 the yardmaster's phone rings: The Mohawk dispatcher reports that New York, Susquehanna & Western SY1 is on the move westward to Onondaga, and Mohawk is asking for a route into the yard. A quick look at the consist paperwork confirms 21 cars today off SY1, a challenge for a yard where no single track holds more than 11 cars. The decision: SY1 will enter on the South Runner, back off half its train through the interlocking onto the East Lead, and drop the balance ahead on the South Runner. The motive power will then take the North Runner to the fuel facility. By noon, he's put away.

While SY1 has been doing his work, the M&E ME1 has headed back from Iroquois "light" (engine only, no cars) and has entered the yard and North Runner at CP 280, heading to the Park Yard to pick up two cars for Euclid. With an air test quickly completed, ME1's crew contacts its dispatcher in Morristown, N.J., for track authority on the M&E, then the yardmaster for permission to depart, and finally the Conrail Mohawk dispatcher to get the route and signal through CP 282.

Between the North and South Runners are the two subsidiary yards which collectively constitute Onondaga Yard. The four-track Park Yard is accessed off the North Runner, while the three-track Field Yard is reached off the South Runner. The Onondaga engine house and service facility (fuel and MofW storage) is adjacent to CP 280 off the North Runner. Running between the engine house and the service facility is the local industrial track to Cazenovia (more on that later). In addition, a small propane dealer has a spur off the CP 282 interlocking on the north side of the tracks.

YARD OPERATIONS

At 0600 the yard is in pretty good shape, with just the setout from road train COSE (Columbus, Ohio, to Selkirk,

A little past 1200, with SY1's power at the enginehouse and ME1 safely back on its own railroad, ON14 hustles down to the South Runner to work SY1's 21-car setoff. There are seven cars for pickup later by westbound road train SENF (SElkirk-Niagara Falls), seven for SEEL (SElkirk-ELkhart), three cars for ELSE (ELkhart-SElkirk), two destined for local WADE30, and two for M&E's ME2. The SENF block is placed on the East Lead, with the others finding temporary homes on different tracks in the Park Yard.

ON14 has barely completed this task when returning WAON10 is on Onondaga's doorstep. ON10 will drop its 15 cars on the South Runner, using the North Runner for the power to return to the enginehouse.

The fast clock shows 1400 (2 p.m.) as ON14 drops down to work WAON10's train. The big 15-car drop consists of five SENFs for the East Lead, while three for ELSE, two for SEEL, two for the ME2, two cars for local delivery in Onondaga, and a single DE30 car find room in the rapidly filling Park Yard.

A final check will be made on SY1's outbound blocks in the Field Yard to ensure all placarded hazardous material cars are properly buried and spaced (federal regulations on cars carrying hazardous and flammable products place restrictions on where they can be placed in trains). Then the two local delivery cars — a propane car for Niagara Propane and a diesel fuel car for the Onondaga enginehouse storage tanks — are spotted and any empties are returned to the Park Yard.

There's a little breathing room in mid-afternoon as ON14 finishes the local switching. There isn't another train scheduled to work the yard until 1700, when Susquehanna's outbound SY1 will put its train together. But movements will be rapid-fire once the sun sets.

SY1's 18 outbound cars are too long to fit on any single track in Onondaga Yard, so it sits in two pieces on Field Yard-1 and Field Yard-2. The Susquehanna crew doubles its train together, completes an air test, and heads eastward through CP 280, clearing out the Field Yard in the process.

EVENING

At this point it's a few minutes past 1800 (6 p.m.) and the ON20 crew has relieved ON14. Minoa & Euclid's ME2 has been patiently waiting at CP 282 for over an hour to enter the west end of Onondaga Yard. With SY1 now clear, the yardmaster contacts the Mohawk Dispatcher to let ME2 in on the South Runner. ME2 will be leaving four cars on Track 2 in the Field Yard, picking up five cars off Park Yard Track 3 then heading back to CP 282 and M&E trackage.

It's now 1900, and as the train action begins to heat up, Dave's layout lights dim to represent dusk. The two yard light towers are illuminated, providing small pools of light over the east and west yard switch ladders. In between, however, the bulk of the yard is in an inky darkness. Operators at sessions who have held second and third-trick jobs on prototype railroads have commented on how realistically Dave has captured the sinister feel of freight yards at night.

Transfer job WADE30 from DeWitt Yard in East Syracuse is next to arrive. He will drop his 11-car train on the South Runner, fuel the locomotives, then pick up cars to return to DeWitt. ON20 quickly gets into position to switch out DE30's setoff: two NYS&W cars for Field-3; three cars to return to DeWitt on outbound DE30 for Field-2; three cars join the rest of SEEL's pickup on Park-1; and three cars for the Cazenovia Industrial Track get placed on Park-4.

The fast clock keeps ticking and we're approaching the 2045 anticipated arrival of ELSE. One last bit of yard housekeeping for ON20 is to bring six DE30 cars from the Park Yard over to the Field Yard to join the seven DE30s already there. This will position all DE30 cars in one yard for the local's eventual departure.

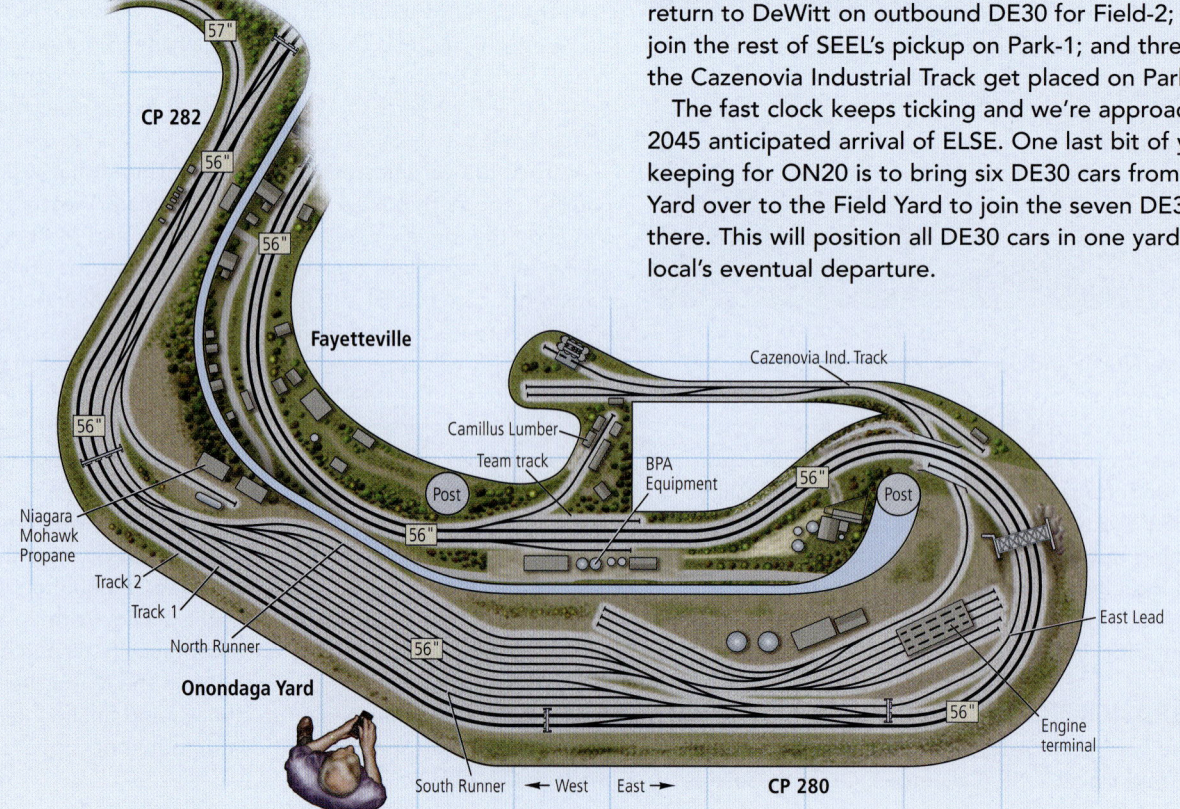

106

Elkhart-Selkirk road train ELSE has a 13-car setoff for Onondaga Yard and will be picking up nine cars out of the Park Yard. Onondaga Yard is quite cramped due to Conrail downsizing in the 1970s and '80s, and a big train such as ELSE simply cannot fit in the yard. Thankfully, tonight there are no westbound trains scheduled on the Onondaga Cutoff for the next couple of hours, so the Mohawk Dispatcher can let ELSE work off Track 1 at CP 280 while a number of eastbound intermodal trains pass on Track 2.

COSE generally arrives at Onondaga around dawn and makes a setout before heading east. The yardmaster and dispatcher have communicated, and COSE will be making its setout off the main line at CP 280. Here engineer Rich Wisneski talks to his conductor on the radio.

ELSE arrives with a consist of four blocks of cars. Block 2 is to be set off at Onondaga; blocks 1, 3, and 5 go through. The pickup at Onondaga will be block 4. This requires ELSE to set off block 2 in the yard, return to the main to pick up block 3 (blocks need to be in numerical order), back into the yard for the block 4 pickup, and finally back to the main to pick up block 5.

At 2300, DE30's power is ready to head out of the engine facility and double its train together. He'll depart out of the Field Yard with 13 cars, including two on the head end to switch out at the BPA siding in Fayetteville.

As DE30 does his double on the east end of the Field, ON20 begins to work the ELSE setoff from the west end. There are seven NYS&W interchange cars among the 13 set off by ELSE, and those seven will be staying in the Field. The other six cars from the setoff are moved up to the Park Yard: four for WAON10 and two for tomorrow's DE30.

Around 2330 ON20 will tie down on the North Runner next to the yard office for dinner during a short respite in the action. The yard is now in good shape with the next train scheduled to be SENF shortly after midnight with a pickup only off the East Lead.

At about a quarter past midnight (0015), Selkirk-Niagara Falls SENF appears at CP 280. SENF's 11-car pickup is on the East Lead and will become its block 2. The Mohawk Dispatcher lines the route onto the South Runner, and SENF holds onto its block 1 cars, leaving the balance on Main Track 1 east of CP 280.

As SENF works its pickup, ON20 has tied onto SEEL's 12-car pickup in the Park Yard and prepares to shove these onto the East Lead once it is cleared off by SENF. The parallel crossovers at CP 280 will be put to good use, as SENF returning to Main Track 1 is snaking through the interlocking at the same time as ON20 is backing SEEL's pickup from the Park Yard to the East Lead.

The need for ON20 to expeditiously get the SEEL pickup to the East Lead is revealed as the Mohawk Dispatcher announces SEEL, closely following on the heels of the departing SENF. SEEL (SElkirk-ELkhart) will pick up those 12 cars off the East Lead as its outbound block 3 and set off 10 cars as inbound block 3, also to the East Lead.

Similar to the earlier SENF move, SEEL is lined for the South Runner. It enters, holding onto blocks 1, 2, and inbound 3, then makes the pickup of outbound block 3 off the East Lead. After reversing back to his train at CP 280 and dropping outbound block 3 with his train, inbound 3 is dropped on the East Lead.

A reverse again to his standing train at CP280, an air test, and SEEL is on the move westward via the South Runner to CP 282 and Main Track 1.

COMPLETING THE CYCLE

With all the night's comings and (mainly) goings, the Park and Field Yards feel almost empty. This will be short-lived as ON20 moves to the East Lead to retrieve SEEL's 10-car setout; another 10 cars will soon be set out by eastbound COSE.

It's closing in on 0400 as ON20 lugs the 10 cars off the East Lead over to the South Runner and Field Yard. Four interchange cars are added to the other NYS&W cars in the Field. Six other cars get yarded up in the Park Yard: two each for the Minoa & Euclid ME1 to deliver to Iroquois Paper, the M&E to bring back to Euclid, and for local delivery by Conrail in Onondaga.

At 0500 the COlumbus-SElkirk COSE comes to a halt on Main Track 1 at CP 280. With a 10-car setout and no pickup, COSE will cut off from the balance of his train and back the 10 cars onto the South Runner. Quickly back onto his train, COSE is on the move eastward following an air test just before 0600.

The crew of ON20 makes their last moves before being relieved by ON14 at 0600, bringing an end to our 24-hour visit to Onondaga Yard. The finishing touches are put on local WAON10, with cars for Fayetteville customers at the head, followed by DeWitt cars and a shoving platform (former caboose) on the rear.

To recap the action at Onondaga Yard over the past 24 hours:
• 4 Conrail road trains picking up and/or setting off: SENF, SEEL, ELSE, COSE
• 4 Conrail local trains originating, terminating or turning: outbound WAON10, inbound WAON10, inbound WADE30, outbound WADE30
• 2 NYS&W interchange trains: inbound SY1, outbound SY1
• 2 Minoa & Euclid interchange trains: inbound ME1, outbound ME1, inbound ME2, outbound ME2

CHAPTER TEN

A FINAL LOOK AT YARDS

By now, you have been exposed to much of what makes railroad yards work. You've seen different examples and read discussions by experts on component parts of yards and what purposes they serve. I hope the previous chapters have inspired you to take a renewed look at modeling yard designs and operations.

Opposite page: Traveling for the hobby is fun, and operating on different railroads is a great experience. It's a privilege to help bring a model railroad to life for those that created it. Tom Schmieder waits at the big yard at Bakersfield, Calif., on the La Mesa Model Railroad Club's incredible HO scale Tehachapi Pass layout in San Diego on November 2, 2018.

Sharing the hobby with younger people is not just important but rewarding and fun. Teddy (right) and Pete Abeles switch Euclid Yard on the Onondaga Cutoff in 2020.

Our goal is to emulate the prototype, and we've looked at the design and development of yards through history and across the country. We've examined how to ensure a modeled yard is functional despite the need for selective compression. Operators and builders alike can now see some of the pitfalls we encounter, and hopefully I've provided ideas for avoiding mistakes and overcoming challenges.

Perhaps most importantly, we've seen inspiring modeling from some of the hobby's finest railroads. The evidence is everywhere — not only are we in a Golden Age of modeling railroading: railroading is a historic industry!

Let's take a final look at the railroad yard: a place where equipment, infrastructure and people all intersect to provide critical services to all. Traffic mixes and is sorted, locomotives come, get serviced, and depart again. Men and women arrive, work together, move trains across the continent, and then return home. Yards have always been places that tie a railroad together, where you see camaraderie in action and bear witness to the success that comes from working together.

And that is the next-level lesson for us as modelers: Our yards, regardless of size, become a place on our miniature railroads where that same camaraderie exists. Our creations are not just models of the track, equipment, and structures — they also provide a stage for the dynamic interaction between human beings and the machines they operate to keep the railroad moving. In designing and operating model yards, be aware of the "big picture" items they support.

Our yards allow us the privilege of owning something that actively brings people closer together. We can agree or disagree in the operational process, but even in disagreement we are defining connections. Yards give us a mission that is more important than the different approaches we have, and the common vision of a well-run yard can be a stepping stone to larger themes in life: belonging, trusting, cooperation, resilience, patience, persistence, and the satisfaction that comes from building something in service of something larger — something others can use, too. The best is still yet to come.

FURTHER READING AND RESOURCES

Abeles, Dave. *The Model Railroader's Guide to Signals and Interlockings.* Kalmbach Media, 2021.
Armstrong, John H. *The Railroad: What it Is, What it Does.* Simmons-Boardman, 1994.
Armstrong, John. *Track Planning for Realistic Operation, Third Edition.* Kalmbach, 1998.
Block Line magazine (Tri-State Chapter NRHS). Vol. 9, No. 5, October 1981
Chubb, Bruce A. *How to Operate your Model Railroad.* Kalmbach, 1977.
Daily, Don. "Around the clock at Frankfort Yard," *Model Railroad Planning,* 1996
Koester, Tony. *Realistic Model Railroad Design.* Kalmbach, 2004.
Koester, Tony. *Steam & Diesel Locomotive Servicing Terminals.* Kalmbach Media, 2018.
Kraft, Edwin. "Railroading's Hidden Half: The Yard," Part 1: "What Yards Do and How They Work," *Trains,* June 2002; Part 2: "Yards of the future," July 2002.
Operations SIG (special interest group), National Model Railroad Association. www.opsig.org
Trains.com. Track plan database: www.trains.com/mrr/how-to/track-plan-database/
Sperandeo, Andy. *The Model Railroader's Guide to Freight Yards.* Kalmbach, 2004.
Wilson, Jeff. *The Model Railroader's Guide to Intermodal Equipment and Operations.* Kalmbach, 1999.
Wilson, Jeff. *The Railroading Handbook.* Kalmbach Media, 2022.

South Kearny Yard in northern New Jersey has always been an important one to its owner, just as it is today. Built by the Pennsylvania, today it is split between CSX, the Port Authority of New York and New Jersey, and NJ Transit. Here, the sun sets as a CSX double-stack train departs for the River Line and a western connection on March 18, 2023 while NJT works in the background at its Meadows Maintenance Complex, the primary shops maintaining its fleet of passenger cars and locomotives. Russell Sullivan